PRESSING FORWARD

PRESSING FORWARD

MY LIFE AS A
BATON ROUGE COMMUNITY
PIONEER

PRESS L. ROBINSON SR.

LOUISIANA STATE UNIVERSITY PRESS
BATON ROUGE

Published by Louisiana State University Press
lsupress.org

Copyright © 2024 by Louisiana State University Press
All rights reserved. Except in the case of brief quotations used in articles or reviews, no part of this publication may be reproduced or transmitted in any format or by any means without written permission of Louisiana State University Press.

DESIGNER: Barbara Neely Bourgoyne
TYPEFACE: Arno Pro

Jacket photograph: *Advocate* File Photo.

Cataloging-in-Publication Data are available from the Library of Congress.

ISBN 978-0-8071-8281-9 (cloth: alk. paper)
ISBN 978-0-8071-8364-9 (pdf)
ISBN 978-0-8071-8363-2 (epub)

CONTENTS

FOREWORD, *by Charles Vincent* vii
AUTHOR'S NOTE xi

1. The Formative Years 1
2. Family Matters 17
3. Going to College 30
4. Home Sweet Home, or Acclimation to Baton Rouge 50
5. Early Years at Southern 60
6. Wings beyond the University 72
7. My Waltz with the Courts 115
8. Challenges, Challenges, Challenges 132
9. Southern Administrative Career 150
10. Other System Positions 157
11. Life after Southern 172

SOURCES 179
INDEX 185

Photographs follow page 98.

FOREWORD

In this book, Press L. Robinson Sr. shares an honest and riveting account of his life as an education pioneer and community activist. The son of sharecropping parents in rural South Carolina, Robinson may have seemed destined to continue his parents' difficult and backbreaking way of life. However, the unfolding of his life story demonstrates that education can be a life-changing agent. Despite her limited high school education, Robinson's mother valued schooling. She insisted that her son attend class every day and for full school terms, contrary to the wishes of the white landowner whose fields the family tended. Despite his lack of exposure to many of life's benefits while living on the farm, young Robinson's views were gradually transformed as he advanced through junior and senior high school and became a close friend of Fred Bell Jr. Bell's father was a districtwide Boy Scouting executive, and his mother was well educated. Neither they nor Fred ever doubted that Fred would one day attain a college education. The influence of Bell's college-bound mentality, combined with his own mother's ardent desire for her son to be educated, encouraged Robinson to dream of personal advancement through education.

A proud graduate of Wilson High School in his hometown of Florence, South Carolina, Robinson earned a scholarship to the prestigious Morehouse College in Atlanta, Georgia. There, he succeeded in earning a bachelor's degree with honors in chemistry. With that background, Howard University in Washington, DC, awarded him a graduate assistantship to study for a master's degree. But Robinson wanted more and earned a PhD in physical chemistry and physics, which led him to Southern University in Baton Rouge, Louisiana.

While teaching chemistry at Southern for thirty years, Robinson developed a strong interest in community and political service. He gained public office in two distinct positions—on the Democratic State Central Committee and the East Baton Rouge School Board. When it became clear that election to the school board was not possible for a Black person under the at-large ward system in place at the time, Robinson filed a federal suit to alter the ward system to single-member election districts. Settlement of that suit produced three majority-Black election districts, one of which made Robinson the first elected Black school board member in East Baton Rouge Parish. Having made history, Robinson broke another barrier when he became the first Black president of the East Baton Rouge School Board. He served in that capacity for three terms.

This farm boy turned educator and successful public servant did not stop there in his achievements. Robinson was instrumental in many civic and grassroots initiatives that determined the character of Baton Rouge and had a direct bearing on the day-to-day lives of Black residents. In the higher education arena, Robinson became a Southern University administrator known for his honesty, straight-shooting demeanor, adherence to policy, and being a man of his word. He served in administrative capacities at the Baton Rouge, Shreveport, and New Orleans campuses and finished his career as chancellor at Southern University in New Orleans following a stint as system vice president for academic and student affairs.

Now retired from education and public service, Robinson continues to fight for the rights of Black Americans, especially in voting rights and redistricting. He is the lead plaintiff in *Robinson v. Landry* (formerly *Robinson v. Ardoin*), the current congressional redistricting case in Louisiana.

Robinson's story is not about his destinations, but his journeys to reach them. Robinson rose from no hope to hope, and from hope to hard work to right action and an educational career beyond expectations. What began as a boyhood venture against the odds turned into a journey of history for

FOREWORD

Blacks in Louisiana. This book is a balanced combination of his accomplishments, belief system, and perspectives on his life's body of work. It is an inspiration to anyone desiring to improve their own community and the future of its residents.

CHARLES VINCENT
retired professor of history, Southern University Baton Rouge
Director of the Mwalimu Institute

AUTHOR'S NOTE

People have often told me that I should write my life story. To this I would usually respond that my life experiences were not significant enough to interest anyone, and I'd have no idea which parts to write about, or how to write about them.

However, after retiring in 2005—and after reviewing a friend's memoir, and hearing that friend say, once again, that my personal stories were worth sharing—I found myself finally putting my life experiences in writing. Even if the stories I chose to include are unimportant to anyone other than myself, here they are. I hope that they will say something about my historical and spiritual heritage.

PRESSING FORWARD

CHAPTER 1

The Formative Years

When I was born—on August 2, 1937, between Claussen and Florence, South Carolina—times were better than, but also not too different from, those of my ancestors and perhaps my parents. I wish I'd written stories about our family's early life when my parents and older relatives were still alive. They could have shared with me their knowledge about slavery. I strongly suspect that my maternal and paternal grandparents were slaves, yet I do not know that for a fact. My parents, who were likely born around 1916–1917, did not experience slavery directly. Unfortunately, neither my mother nor my father ever talked about their parents or other ancestors. Perhaps it was too painful to talk about, and they wanted to forget. Consequently, I never knew the names of my grandparents on either side.

A journey into the past through *Ancestry.com* yielded little information about my grandparents. I had hoped to find information about them; such information is readily available for the ancestors of white people. Truthfully, I believed that I would not find much, for I understood that chronicling the lives of Black people was considered unimportant, especially in the segregated South.

History tells us that when the enslaved people of the South gained freedom, many of these individuals did not know what to do or where to go, so they stayed on the plantations where they were. Many became sharecroppers—farm workers whose landowners took a part of each crop as wages and charged them for farming and/or food expenses. Sharecropping was a big improvement over slavery because sharecroppers could decide they didn't want to do it anymore and leave; enslaved people could not.

My dad was a sharecropper, yet the two of us never talked about how he became one. What did he have to do to become one? Were there any other choices for him? What was the crop value share agreement between him and the landowner? When was the sharecropper agreement made?

I often wonder how my father and mother met. Was their marriage arranged, or was it their choice? My ancestry research shows that my parents married on November 15, 1936. There was not quite enough time for an average pregnancy period of nine months before I was born. Was my mother pregnant before marriage, or was I born before the normal gestation period? Did our name "Robinson" come from an enslaver? What about Mom's people, and their surname "Isaiah" (or Isaih)? What plantation (called "townships" in the official records during slavery) did my ancestors live and work on? Where did my ancestors come from?

I asked my dad where he and my mom got the name Press, and he told me that my name is the same as a cousin of mine. He didn't seem to know where the cousin got his name.

Both my mother and my father were from large families, and I got to know all of their sisters and brothers, each of whom was kind to my immediate family. Family was the backbone unit of life in those days, working in concert with church and school to form an encouraging and sustaining framework for living—not necessarily living well, but surviving.

Adults supported each other, and every adult helped raise the children. As the saying goes, it takes a village to raise a child, and in my experience, the village was real. In my presence, my mother and father told other adults that they had permission to discipline me any time they observed me misbehaving. As further incentive to behave myself, if my parents learned that an outsider had punished me, the result might be a worse disciplining at home. That kind of "village oversight" and a strong belief in religion led to life at my parents' house as one based on honesty, respect for myself and others, and hard work. It was a natural form of love. As the Bible says, "Train up a child in the way he should go, and when he is old he will not depart from it."

THE FORMATIVE YEARS

* * *

One day, I suddenly realized that I was alive. I was about six years old. This is my earliest sense of discovering and being aware of myself. I was living with my mother, father, and a cousin, Ruthie Lee, who grew up in our family as my half-sister.

My childhood was in the 1940s. In Florence County we got to experience four distinct seasons every year. Winter was especially enjoyable, because it sometimes snowed at Christmas. As the snow came down, it would collect on the railings of the house porch as pure, clear, clean crushed ice, from which my mother made the best snow-ices ever. She knew just how to combine the ice with vanilla extract, sugar, and other ingredients into a delicious treat that no one else in the family knew how to do. There were few opportunities to find that type of treat. We otherwise had to settle for cakes and pies on special occasions.

Mom was a sweet person who got along with just about anyone, but she also had her favorites, the names of whom I can no longer remember. I am not sure how she managed it all, but her daily chores included preparing breakfast for the family, working in the fields until perhaps 10:30 a.m., heading to the house to prepare dinner (called lunch nowadays), heading back to the fields after dinner, and then preparing supper at the end of the day. There was no question that she was a good cook. As far as I knew, she could cook anything.

Dad was the final decision maker—the head of the household—and the most dreaded punisher. So naturally, I tried desperately to avoid angering him. Mom was usually the family disciplinarian, especially where I was concerned. Her discipline was often stern, yet much less onerous than my dad's. Still, she did not believe in sparing the rod. I hated when Mom made me go out and get the switch she would use for my punishment.

She would say, "Go get me a switch, and it better be a good one. You make sure that it's got plenty of give in it." That meant the switch was flexible enough to bend around whatever part of the body she chose to attack, usually the rear end. Man, those types of switches hurt like hell.

When we no longer worked the farm, my mom became a domestic in the homes of Florence's white elites. I hated her working for those people, yet understood that the job options were slim to none for Black women. Mom was the angel in my life, even though I knew Dad cared for me deeply.

Dad advanced only through the sixth grade in formal education. Mom finished high school and thus showed more appreciation for education, which would be my escape from a life of bare existence or, as we said, "making do." Still, that sixth-grade education proved to work wonders for my dad, as he could handle numbers, which we referred to as "figures," well. Thus, he managed money and measurements around the farm efficiently, and rarely found himself outfoxed.

Dad was an excellent shot with a .22 rifle, making him a successful hunter of local wild game and a superb slaughterer of rattlesnakes. Shooting the snakes in the head from behind seemed to be one of his favorite pastimes. Snakes can attack by jumping backward. Dad knew it and often talked about it. And still he preferred shooting a snake from behind with his single-shot rifle.

My dad was well liked by most people, and he was considered someone to consult about life's ups and downs. Farm work did not leave much time for extracurricular activities. Still, Dad found time to be an active Prince Hall Mason, and much of his life's values resulted from the Freemasonry doctrines of devotion to fellowship, moral discipline, and mutual assistance. I inherited many of my innate doctrines from my dad's Masonic beliefs and practices.

I recall how he would conceal some of the Masons' rituals, customs, and activities from me and from the public. I think the Masons were his prize organization outside of the church. He was always proud to talk about them and what they were doing in the community. More than that, he loved getting together with his fellow fraternity members.

Ruthie Lee was six years older than me and often had the responsibility to oversee my daily activities. She never spent a lot of time playing with me, nor did she allow me to be in her immediate presence. But I knew she was around and could receive her help when needed. And when my parents were away, Ruthie Lee took care of me. I can remember how proud I was when she broke the news of her marriage to her boyfriend, Eddie

Williams. I'd known she had a boyfriend, who came to see her now and then. It had not occurred to me that he would be taking her away.

Ruthie Lee and Eddie moved to Brooklyn, New York. Their move occurred about the time my parents and I changed residences, from what I called the "house in the woods" to what I called the "house beside the highway." I was alone, but soon just as happy as I could be, not missing Ruthie Lee very much.

In time, Ruthie Lee and Eddie had a daughter, Margie. Lynn and Edith followed in relatively rapid succession. Brooklyn was a long way away, and we only heard from Ruthie Lee and her family sparingly. But Mom knew how to make contact with them and did so when the need arose.

The "house in the woods" belonged to a landowner. This house, located miles from a highway, was, as far as I was concerned, in the woods. But it was not literally in the woods—it was surrounded by fields used for planting crops. The woods surrounded the fields and were an acceptable distance away from the house. The house consisted of boards that separated us from outside. There was no such thing as insulation, and often you could see outside from within the house through the cracks between boards. The times when we noticed the cracks most were in fall and winter.

Winters were frigid, and so was the inside of the house. All we had to give us any warmth, other than our clothing, was a wood-burning heater usually located a few feet from the wall in the middle of one room of the house. Boy, did I hate the duty of being the first one up in the winter mornings to light the heater's fire. Our beds were so warm and cozy, covered with the heavy quilts made by my mother and her circle of friends. The fire-starting process was not too bad if you could get it going quickly, but that was not always the case.

It was amazing to me that, at night, I would go to bed alone, and when I awoke in the morning, our cat was next to me under the covers. I would think, how did the cat do that, and when? I never found out, but I knew we'd both had a good night's sleep.

The thing I hated most about those cold winters was having to use outside bathroom amenities. We had an outhouse, which was a wooden building with a seat over a hole or pit in the ground. The amenities weren't any better during other seasons of the year, but at least we didn't have to deal with the chill of winter.

We had an ever-present concern about exposing ourselves to critters, such as spiders, snakes, and rodents, in the outhouse. Spiders were the most feared and the most likely. We knew that some spiders, such as the black widow and brown recluse, possessed venom that attacked nerve cells and caused immense pain. I could never be sure when one of these spiders might be hiding beneath the toilet seat.

We had many chores around the farmhouse, most of them repetitive, adhering to a regular schedule. The *Farmers' Almanac* was the go-to source for those who didn't know or couldn't remember when certain activities had to be done. One of the most pleasant things I had to do every day was milk the cow. There was a trick to it. You had to learn how to eject the milk from the cow's udder while carefully watching her "body English." During milking, cows often kicked with their hind legs, and such blows could cause serious injury.

Although milking cows was something I didn't mind doing, I seriously hated the chore of transforming the sweet milk into buttermilk. The usual process for making butter was putting milk in a jar and shaking it until butter formed. That process could take several hours a day, over several days. To me it seemed to take forever. My mother thought it was my job to make the buttermilk, no questions asked, although sometimes I would get relief from her or Ruthie Lee.

That was the best-tasting milk, and it made great buttermilk. We drank buttermilk alone as a beverage or with hot cornbread. I often partake of store-bought buttermilk and cornbread to this day.

We had only one milk cow, but she gave more milk than a family of four could consume. Because the cow needed relief from the milk pressure in her udder, sometimes we would simply let the milk fall to the ground because we had enough to cook with or to drink.

Our favorite dinner dishes, especially on Sundays, were fried or stewed chicken with rice. Mom didn't think anything of telling me, "Boy, go outside and catch me a chicken." That meant I had to run the chicken down, either wring or pull its neck off, soak it in hot water, and pluck its feathers.

I always seemed to get the dirty jobs. The chickens never cooperated, which made catching one a huge exercise. But I always managed to catch the chicken, even though it may have taken many tries and considerable time. Once the chicken was caught, killed, and cleaned, the next phase of preparation—cooking—produced a great result. I can remember thinking just how delicious properly prepared chicken can be.

Ruthie Lee and I were very happy to have fried chicken for dinner, except when the preacher came around. Being last to get served sometimes meant not getting any chicken, depending on how much the good preacher ate. In such a case, Mom would say to us, "Eat your vegetables." It was common knowledge that you dare not complain, and certainly not in front of the preacher. If you did complain, look out for the discipline sure to follow, ranging from a tongue lashing to a whipping.

But through this I learned that there was a "pecking order" in life. Pecking orders were to be observed at all times, along with respect for certain persons, your elders, and your cohorts. My parents and the community also reared me to be humble, thankful, and respectable. My elders encouraged me to believe that I was no better than anyone else and that no one else was better than me. I was to treat every person as I would want them to treat me, no matter their station in life.

Another repetitious farm routine was the killing of the hogs. This event usually took one to two days, depending on the number of hogs killed and how much help was available. As was the case with chickens, practically every part of the carcass, other than the hair, had a purpose. A hog yielded ham, bacon, pork sausage, pig lips and feet, hogshead cheese, chitterlings, and cracklings (pork skins). I am amazed when I visit the grocery store today and see all of these items enjoyed by the public, not just by farmers.

Folks would come from miles around to help with the hog killings and to receive their bounties of one or more of the items produced. In many cases, their "pay" was simply "you help me when I make my killing." Again, the village was on display. After the slaughter, the sausage was made, the cracklings were cooked, and the chitterlings (leftover hog intestines not used as sausage casings) were thoroughly cleaned. Our next concern was storage.

Refrigeration was not a means of preservation generally available to sharecroppers. When we were finally able to own refrigeration equipment, it was an icebox kept cool by blocks of ice purchased from the iceman. I don't remember when we got our first electric refrigerator with a freezer. But the freezing capacity of that appliance was still much too small to accommodate the volume of meat generated by butchering a hog.

The prevailing method of preserving meat was to pack it in salt and hang it in the smokehouse. We would wash the salt off the meat to the extent desired before cooking. Sometimes the meat was smoked before storage, and thus it required less salt. These processes ensured that we had meat to eat year-round. Feasting on beef, instead of pork and chicken, was rare, since we had no money to buy beef, and slaughtering a cow for food was seldom done. We owned our cows for their milk.

In those days, if you wanted to leave the farm and go somewhere, you had three options: walk where you wanted to go; ride the back of a mule or in a mule-drawn wagon; or be lucky enough to have someone with a car pick you up. Riding a mule was not bad transportation and was much better than walking. If you needed to carry multiple items, the wagon was the way to go. Not many Black people had cars, so that likelihood was more than remote. These few options meant that we did not leave the farm very often. Fortunately, we grew or raised almost everything we needed to eat, including corn, potatoes, vegetables, chickens, and hogs. Coupled with an occasional visit to the general store, our food needs were covered. Sometimes we received goods through delivery by the landowner.

The sharecropping system came about following the Civil War, when formerly enslaved people sought jobs, and planters/landowners sought laborers. This form of agricultural labor still exists today and may continue for a long time to come. Since Black sharecroppers usually did not have any money until the sale of their harvests, the landowner charged the amounts for various items—such as seeds, tools, and food, plus rent for living quarters—to the sharecropper's account. When the harvest sold, the sharecropper paid on the account from his proportion of the proceeds. My dad had no choice about which crops we planted and sold, a fact I did not know until I was twelve or thirteen years old.

We planted cotton, corn, and tobacco on the commercial side of sharecropping. People like us, who did not have large families, had to subscribe to the philosophy "I help you with your planting and harvesting, and you help me with mine"—another example of the village concept in action. You might be surprised how well that philosophy worked. It also provided an opportunity for families and friends to visit each other. Such cooperative ventures could last one or two days or stretch into one or two weeks.

When I got older—my dad was still sharecropping at the time—I learned that sometimes Black people could not successfully clear their credited accounts at the harvest sale time. The sharecropping system was terrible for Blacks because it created and increased poor laborers' debt to plantation owners. After a while, the sharecropper could owe so much money to the landowner that they had to give them all of the money they made from their cotton and/or tobacco harvest—a position not, in the end, different from slavery. I am not sure if my family was ever in that situation. If so, my dad did not talk about it.

I could not understand why Black people thought our family had money in our post-sharecropper days. It might have been because, starting in about 1940, Dad always had a car. His first—a 1936 Ford—was somewhat old, but he maintained a relatively recent vehicle thereafter.

One car, in particular, was simply beautiful, and in comparison with the first car, it was magnificent. It was a maroon 1947 four-door Ford and was "tight as a bell" compared to the 1936 car. Maroon or burgundy is still one of my favorite colors, especially in cars and clothes. I don't know how we afforded it, but the dealer repeatedly drove that car out to our farm, probably for over a year, until Dad finally bought it. But the pride and joy of our fleet, as far as I was concerned, was the 1951 Ford, light blue with a white top. It was the only one of our cars that I had the privilege of driving (not counting the times when Dad would sit me in his lap and let me steer).

I remember that the blue-and-white Ford caused a lot of trouble in our household, because someone informed Mom that they saw our car parked at another house every day. I don't have to tell you what Mom's conclusion was. She was wrong, but it became necessary for my dad to prove to her satisfaction that he was not spending time with some other woman.

One day when she was fussing about the situation, I reminded her that there was no way that the car reported was Dad's car. How did I know? I knew because I was home from college, I drove Dad to work every day and picked him up, and I therefore had the car all day, every day. But Mom was still getting reports about the blue-and-white Ford parked at that other house.

Finally we concluded that there must be a second blue-and-white Ford in town. I was able to verify that by driving past the other address. Lo and behold, we saw a Ford parked there, identical to ours. What a relief, not only to my mom, but also to me, and later to my dad, after we explained the circumstances. My mom and dad had other disputes, but none that threatened our home as much as the identical car incident.

After two to three years of living on the farm "in the woods," my dad decided to move us to a farm "on the highway." I was pretty pleased about the move, because it allowed me to see who might pass by on the road. I was not old enough to work in the fields yet, and spent my days playing alone in the sandy driveway, in the yard, or under our raised house, sometimes with my dog. Over a day, if I was lucky, I would witness the passage of one or two cars and perhaps a person or two walking, riding a mule, or riding a bicycle. Other times, there was nothing to see until my parents came home.

When I was about ten, those days of leisure were over. I had to join the field workforce and do whatever was necessary: plow the fields, crop tobacco, pick cotton, break corn, fertilize the crops. As kids, we complained about being tired or about the heat when working in the fields; but invariably we would spend much of our lunch break running around in the heat and playing.

One of my most hated farm chores was feeding the hogs. The hog pens were far away from the house because of their smell, and it was hard work toting the feed down from the house to the pens. Perhaps my next most hated task was picking red peppers, which my dad planted a few times when we were farming. What made this chore so distasteful was the burning sensation one developed over the entire body after picking the peppers. Everywhere you touched burned. I strongly encouraged my dad never to plant red peppers again. I do not know if it was my begging him not to or something else, but eventually he relented.

Of the commercial crops (tobacco, cotton, and corn), tobacco and cotton were the most labor intensive. We grew tobacco on five to ten acres by inserting young plants, about eight inches tall, into holes dug by hand, in freshly tilled soil about two feet apart in rows four feet apart. Depending on the soil moisture, adding water to the hole may have been necessary. Keeping the plants healthy throughout the growing season required large amounts of fertilizer and pesticides. Between 100 and 130 days, the plants began to ripen, a process that started at the bottom of the plant and moved upward over time. Croppers removed the leaves individually as they ripened.

Cropping tobacco was a process I hated with a passion. On the farm, you worked from sunrise to sunset. The leaves would be wet with dew in the mornings or with rain—as a result, the cropper was wet too—and by 9 or 10 a.m., the sun would be beaming down without mercy. While the croppers removed the ripened tobacco leaves, groups of people—usually women—were at the barn, stringing the leaves with twine onto sticks and then hanging them to cure.

This curing process allowed the leaves to slowly oxidize, producing chemical changes. We used flue-cured methods of aging, where the flues heated the tobacco without exposing it to smoke. The process called for slowly raising the temperature throughout the curing. This method took about a week, required continuous attention, and resulted in tobacco that was high in sugar and medium to high in nicotine.

Cotton was planted in the spring—sometimes as early as February in warm-weather areas and as late as June in cold-weather areas. Plowing the land into rows formed firm seedbeds for planting. We dropped small clumps of seeds into little trenches or furrows in each row, covered them with soil, and spaced them at regular intervals. Keeping the grass and weeds from overtaking the growing cotton plants required extreme efforts. One of those efforts was "chopping cotton" by removing the grass and weeds by hand with a hoe, usually several times per growing season, one row at a time. Another involved plowing the areas between the rows, thus throwing soil onto the roots of the plants while smothering the grass and weeds.

By August or September, the cotton was ready to pick. Harvesting by hand, each picker had his or her sack, on his or her knees or bent over, picking the seed cotton from the burrs attached to the plant stems. An average picker could pick between 100 and 150 pounds of cotton a day, and some pickers as much as 200 pounds a day. I never managed to break the 100 pound-a-day mark until the last day I ever picked cotton. I was proud of reaching that sacred level, but prouder still that I no longer had to pick cotton.

Cotton, even more so than tobacco, required loads of pesticides to fight bugs such as boll weevils (or bollworms), and it was necessary to apply them by hand. To maintain the soil nutrients required large amounts of fertilizer, which were also hand applied. But of all of the labor-intensive chores needed to produce cotton, the ones I disliked most were picking and then chopping the grass and weeds. A typical cotton season consisted of ten to fifteen acres of plants.

Growing corn (maize), the yellow- or white-ear variety, required a long, frost-free, and warm growing season. Planting corn seeds occurred annually around May 15. The crop was best planted in blocks of short rows instead of long, single rows, because corn relies on wind to pollinate its flowers. Seeds were planted about 1 inch deep, 4 to 6 inches apart in rows that were about 30 to 36 inches apart.

Corn required some fertilizer, again applied by hand, but nothing close to the amount of fertilizer for tobacco and cotton. The most labor-intensive intermediate chore was thinning the young plants when they were about three to four inches tall. After thinning they were 8 to 12 inches apart in a row, and the occasional weeding of the crop (another hand exercise) was required. The crop was ready for harvest when the ears' tassels began to turn brown and the cobs started to swell. The kernels would be full and milky. To harvest the corn, we pulled the ears downward and twisted to take them off the stalk—one ear on one plant at a time. We usually planted at least ten acres of corn, most of which we fed to the hogs and mules.

I mention these farming activities because they required the most attention and work during the summer months, when there was no school. School typically began after Labor Day and ended around May 15. This schedule was deliberate so as to accommodate the agricultural calendar. I had to work on the farm, just like everyone else, from about May 15 to Labor Day, no questions asked and no excuses made. There were no farming activities from which I was exempt.

I recall one incident that shows how simple things were in those days and how we appreciated the littlest things. On one of Daddy's tobacco market trips, he came home with a new-sounding horn on our car—a horn that sounded loud and clear, not the old *beep, beep*. That was an occasion for celebration, because it was something new and different. We were proud of ourselves and of our new horn. When you don't have much, every little bit is something to cherish.

Another example of simple joy was when my dad, with a single shot, killed a massive rattlesnake with his .22 rifle and when he used that same rifle for hunting squirrels and came home with a squirrel in every pocket. Boy, did Mom know how to cook those squirrels—that was good eating. There was almost nothing better than squirrel and gravy over rice at dinner or supper, or with grits for breakfast.

One of the more embarrassing incidents in my life happened when I was about ten or twelve years old. I got myself caught between the back of a mule and the top of the mule's stable. I could not keep the mule I was riding from entering the stable, and I could not get off his back quickly enough. Luckily, I did not sustain any severe visible injury to my midsection. I never told my parents about it, but I believe that I have some stomach and back repercussions from that episode even today.

At that point, I was attending Hopewell Elementary School. Thanks to my mother, I attended school every day, all term, from the age of six in 1943 to thirteen in 1950. This may seem to be no big deal, but it definitely was one. My mother insisted that my father inform our landlord that I would be attending school regularly and that I could work in the fields only as school attendance allowed. Somehow, my dad mustered up the courage to do just that. I don't know how much resistance he may have received from the landlord, but I went to school every day. Once we moved from the farm to the city, regular school attendance was no longer an issue requiring special attention.

Some of the family members in my age group did not have that kind of resolve from their parents. They did not attend school every day, and they eventually dropped out of school without finishing their education. The sad part of that story is that their livelihoods either stayed at the level of their parents or barely rose above it. I am not mocking their lives, but rather pointing out that things could have been so much better for them if they had had more education. My life is not extraordinary, but it is far above the way we lived when I was a child and teenager.

During elementary school, I skipped a grade in our little two-room building due to my advanced learning. I suppose one could call what I learned "advanced" only as it applied to Black schools in South Carolina. Our books consisted of used hand-me-downs from white students. Many of the textbooks were old and often contained the names of the previous white owners. I knew that was not what should have been, but I understood that white people didn't care whether we Blacks learned anything or got an education. They preferred that we did not.

In the 1940s and 1950s, white people still considered Black people as "their property" in many ways. We were "nothing." I was lucky to have dedicated teachers who cared about us, often lived in our communities, and taught us as much as they could, sometimes more than what was in those old textbooks. Those books were not only old, but also were carefully selected to exclude information that acknowledged or honored Blacks.

We had no electricity in those days, so I studied by the light of an oil lamp, which was inadequate. I believe that doing so resulted in my developing or aggravating an existing case of astigmatism. As a consequence, I suffered severe and prolonged bouts of headaches, which made walking, playing, working, or simply living very unpleasant. Can you imagine riding the back of a mule with your head aching? This went on for two or three years.

THE FORMATIVE YEARS

My parents did not believe me about the severity and repetition of my headaches, so it took some time before they sought the advice of an eye doctor. I am sure the delay was because a doctor's visit only happened as a last resort, since we had little money to visit a doctor. I believe it was a recommendation from my elementary school teacher, Ms. Holloway, that finally led to my seeing a doctor about those headaches. At ten years old, I got my first pair of eyeglasses. The headaches went away, and I still wear glasses every day.

We finally got electricity, an electric refrigerator, and a washing machine about two or three years before leaving the farm. Before that, we had to rely on the iceman to keep food cool, not cold; and we had to wash our clothes by hand, and do everything else during the day or by lamplight. We had no running water. Instead, we used an outside pump or well. Having a pump for water was a big deal; wells were much more common.

As I and other Black students walked the three to four miles to elementary school each day, a bus routinely passed us, full of white students who thought it was great to make fun of us. We expected that behavior from the white students because we knew their attitudes toward us. White and Black kids between birth and about ten to twelve years of age played together quite regularly. We did not mingle once we reached our teens.

In my own case, the white landowner lived perhaps a quarter of a mile from us, just on the other side of the highway, and I would play with his kids. Suddenly, when we reached the age of ten or twelve, our togetherness ceased. My parents told me that I could not associate with the little white boy anymore, a message I believe came from the landowner through my dad. And the older we got, the further apart we became in our actions and beliefs.

My teacher, Ms. Holloway, taught all grades from first through sixth in two separate classrooms in our two-room school. It was the practice back then for teachers to spend a week at the house of each student every year. I was always afraid of the outcome, given that she'd spend this week in constant contact with my parents. What would she tell them about me, or what would she tell them that I did? I was always happy when that week was over. But to my knowledge, Ms. Holloway never told my parents anything "bad" about me. I was a good little boy.

Now, that is not to say I did not have my moments of missteps. When I was in either the third or fourth grade, my teacher took a pencil and rapped me on the knuckles of my hand. I don't recollect what I did, but that rap on the knuckles hurt so severely that I can even visualize it today. I was also embarrassed, because the discipline occurred in front of the whole class. Worse, I certainly did not want Ms. Holloway to inform my parents that she'd disciplined me, or to have one of my classmates blab about it to someone who would relay it to my parents.

Another blunder of mine concerned my dad's warning one Sunday that I pay special attention to our milk cow while he and Mom went to church. I was not to let her get into the corn garden. Well, I got to playing and completely forgot about the cow, and when I finally remembered my dad's instructions, it was too late. The cow had gotten into the garden and eaten up much of the fresh corn.

When Dad arrived home and saw that the cow had destroyed the corn, he decided to take a belt to me. I only escaped a whipping because I ran and hid under the house until he cooled off. My parents believed in the biblical proverb that if you spared the rod, you spoiled the child. My dad was determined not to spare the rod. But Mom was on my side and gently pleaded with Dad to let me off the hook. It worked, but I never forgot that incident. I became convinced that the axiom about not sparing the rod was true. As an adult, I applied that same rule to my children, and they did so to their children, though perhaps to a lesser degree than I did.

CHAPTER 2

Family Matters

I realize that I have painted a picture of sharecropping that is not very pleasant. Yet even though times were hard and my family did not have much in the way of money and other possessions, we did have practically everything we needed to live, and we made do with whatever we had. We grew vegetables and raised hogs and chickens, which provided meat for the table and was supplemented by the wild game (squirrels, rabbits, coons, and possums) and fish that Dad hunted or caught. He was able to buy, albeit on credit, flour, rice, and other staples that we did not plant or raise. We paid off these and other bills when the crops came in.

Rabbits were easiest to hunt because we could blind them with a vehicle's headlights or other bright light, then shoot them as they sat immobile. Squirrels were harder to get and required Dad to rise early in the morning, before daybreak, to be in place near the hickory or other nut trees before they arrived to feed. Dad's weapon of choice, the single-shot rifle, allowed him to shoot his prey without excessive noise that could drive the squirrels away.

My hunting weapon of choice was a BB gun, and my prey was limited to sparrows. By the time Dad allowed me to use a real gun we no longer lived near good hunting grounds. Now and then, Dad would hunt with a good coon or possum dog. Coon hunting required a special dog whose job was to chase and tree the prey. If the dog was not specially trained, the coon would get the better of him (in other words, beat him up) and get away. We preferred eating coons over possums for two reasons: we considered coons cleaner animals, and they tasted better.

One day I was astonished to learn that a first cousin of mine and her family had found themselves with no food to eat. This was a family of about seven or eight, who usually would have had a garden and other provisions. I was curious about what it looked like not to have food for breakfast. I walked a couple of miles to their house and discovered that breakfast consisted of watermelon and watermelon only. There should have been eggs from the chickens, bacon from the hogs, milk from the cows, and vegetables from the garden. But there was none of that, and we could not understand why. Of course, it was because they had not taken proper measures to ensure that food was available. My dad and others lit into the man of the house, because the situation was avoidable. This story illustrates that no matter what things could be available, they are only available if proactive efforts are made.

Christmas was a fun time for us. Not because of the presents we received, but because three or four of us guys would get together and, on our bicycles, visit our "girlfriends" one at a time. It was fun just being together, laughing and talking while riding, and watching how each of us interacted with "his young lady" and her parents. Some of us did it well; some of us, not so well.

Such a process demanded a lot of bike riding, especially since rural folks did not live very close to each other. It was nothing for us to visit three or four houses, each three to five miles apart. Since it was Christmas, we didn't have to worry about food; everywhere we went, folks urged us to partake of what they had prepared. The girls liked it because they got lots of attention, and everybody in the house knew about our intentions. The parents liked it because they could easily watch whatever was happening.

Another enjoyable time was when we visited other family members or friends we did not see regularly. Both my parents were from large families. Mom had five sisters and one brother, and Dad had eight sisters, thus giving us plenty of people to visit. We did not visit all of them regularly. There were certain family members Mom visited more often, and so did Dad. Because farm work consumed the days, these visits usually occurred in the evenings or on Sundays after church.

When my parents were planning a visit in the evening, there was always the question of what to do with me, since I typically went to bed around 8 p.m. My parents could have left me at home with Ruthie, at least before she married and moved away. But, naturally, I always wanted to go on the visits. So I would pretend to be wide awake when it was time to go—and then I'd fall asleep as soon as I got in the car. It didn't take my parents long to realize what was going on; however, they humored me and took me along.

When we visited a particular family friend of my mom's, we would drive some twenty-five to thirty miles, typically on a Sunday afternoon. Taking such drives allowed Dad to show off just a bit. He would do so by "putting the pedal to the metal" in our 1936 Ford. The normal speed for driving was about 30 to 35 miles per hour. So, when Dad put the pedal to the metal, the Ford would reach 50 miles per hour, and the car would shake violently. Dad only maintained that speed for a short time before he would slow down. We were all game to try the higher speed, but we also felt very uncomfortable with the shaking. Each of the adults would take a turn driving the car at a reduced speed, while the rest of us sat back and allowed the wind to blow through our hair.

Though we never tried such a drive with the 1947 Ford, I bet that no such shaking would have occurred: that car was well built, made of steel, and didn't rattle. We thought going at a high speed was a real adventure. I compared it to the principal at Wilson High School, Mr. Gerard A. Anderson, who never drove his Chevrolet faster than five miles per hour. Meanwhile, there we were, traveling eight to nine times faster. But moving at such a slow speed did not bother Mr. Anderson, and he was content to make the approximately 25-mile trip from Claussen to Florence every Monday through Friday, even though it took about five hours one way.

When Mr. Anderson drove our way, we kids could see him coming down the road. It would take him forever to get to where we were and then forever for him to get out of sight. But as far as I know, he never changed his rate of speed. Often, when we talked about Mr. Anderson and his tortoise speed, I would fantasize that I was driving a car and coming over the hill in the road at 40 miles per hour: flying compared to Mr. Anderson.

I finally got permission to drive our family car, albeit sparingly, when I became a junior in high school.

Dad died of a massive heart attack on March 4, 1989. Ruthie Lee phoned me to let me know he had passed. I had spoken to him the week before, and he seemed to be doing just fine. That past summer, he had visited with me and my wife during the 1988 Democratic Convention in Atlanta, Georgia. His very first airplane ride was his trip back to Florence from Atlanta.

It took me quite a bit of persuasion to get Dad to fly rather than ride the bus. I knew a bus ride would take up an excessive amount of time and also would be exhausting. I think he did not actually enjoy the flight, but he didn't complain about it either. He never flew again. He was a simple man with a sixth-grade education, lots of common sense, and integrity. I have always been proud of him.

Dad was a person who believed in preparation for whatever you were planning to do. He maintained that mentality about his final expenses for his funeral. He had informed me that he had a small savings account in a Florence bank, and that my name was on the account along with Ruthie Lee's.

When I arrived in Florence to plan his funeral, one of my first acts was to verify the amount of money in the account. There wasn't much, but there was more than enough to cover the cost of a lovely funeral. Ruthie Lee and I discussed the account and preliminary plans for the burial. I suggested that we use the money to pay Dad's funeral expenses and split the rest 50/50. We both agreed to that plan of action, and I went about making the arrangements. She didn't offer to assist with any particulars, but it didn't bother me.

When I reached the point of needing to pay the funeral home, I discovered insufficient funds in the savings account to cover the costs. Ruthie Lee had gone to the bank and withdrawn half of the total amount Dad had accumulated. The saying "the love of money is the root of all evil" seems to be a truism. If Ruthie Lee had a problem with my suggestion, she should have told me when I proposed it. Now here I was, having to cover the costs of the funeral with what remained in the account and my personal funds, as well as the airline costs for my wife and me and two weeks of hotel expenses.

So many times I have seen or heard about situations in which family members turn on each other over money. I certainly did not expect it would happen to me and Ruthie Lee. But it did, for the same reason as always: the love of money and its elevation above all else. Sadly, Ruthie Lee died on January 26, 2012. She was buried at Elizabeth Baptist Church near Florence, South Carolina. I never once brought up to her what she had done. I believe that God will always provide.

My family members strongly believed in religion and attended church every Sunday. Dad was a member of Salem Methodist Church, and Mom was a member of Elizabeth Baptist Church. Hence, we attended Methodist services on the first and third Sundays and Baptist services on the second and fourth Sundays. Months with five Sundays found us again in the Methodist Church, for Mom believed that she should adopt the religious traditions of my dad. There was very little difference between the services: we sang the same songs, the preacher preached the same way, and they both had a mixture of Methodists and Baptists in their congregations. There wasn't even a difference in the behavior of the preachers visiting church families for Sunday dinner.

The children hated when the preachers came to eat, because, as I mentioned earlier, we counted on the preachers helping themselves to the last piece of chicken. If it was not the last piece of chicken, it was the last biscuit—always the last of something. Mom would remind us that the preacher ate first, the grownups ate next, and we ate whatever remained. It may not be polite to say that the preacher was greedy; however, that was pretty much the case. But the preacher received special treatment because to us he was more than our spiritual leader. He was the closest thing to God on earth and thus revered.

Because Sunday church services and funerals were the only times we dressed up, Dad had only one suit, and I didn't have one at all. It didn't bother my dad much that he wore the same suit all the time because that was the common practice among the men. Mom didn't have a lot of clothes either, but she was deadly serious about not wearing the same dress in succession or wearing one that was the same as someone else's.

Dad had a good singing voice. He was a regular member of the mixed choir, and he also was a deacon at Salem Methodist. Mom was a member of several ladies' ministries at Elizabeth Baptist. What they did in the church was important and elevated their status above what they experienced outside the church. What they had to say or did meant something to the church members, their friends, and the community.

Preachers, teachers, doctors, and lawyers were the professionals we knew. Children would say they wanted to be one or the other of those professions when they grew up. People would say that I was going to be a preacher, or that I looked like a preacher. Later, when I lived in Baton Rouge, people who did not know me would ask if I was a preacher. I never understood what made them think that. Then again, my parents raised me to believe that religion was not just to be observed on Sunday but every day and in everything that one does.

As a teenager, I particularly enjoyed noting the preacher's theme and following his sermon to see if he developed it in a way that I could relate its meaning to my life and the lives of others. I listened so intently that I could often repeat the theme and some of each sermon's main points. Today, when I think about those teenage years and the preacher's sermons, I believe that my actions formed the basis of my ability to listen well on any issue, no matter the speaker. Because I feel this ability has served me well, I urge others to practice the skills of becoming a better listener.

Given the lifestyle of my family and those with whom we interacted, there was not a lot to do outside of work and church. There were the occasional parties, suppers, and Sunday visits. But everyone looked forward to "going to town" on Saturdays, after working until noon. In town, you would see lots of friends and acquaintances. You would walk back and forth along the two or three streets that comprised the heart of downtown Florence. You could also get the best fish sandwich ever: a simple concoction of a piece of fish between two slices of bakery bread without any condiments. We referred to such bread as "light bread." I don't know what kind of fish it was and can't remember ever asking. In town, we also picked up any necessary household staples we did not produce ourselves.

"Going to town" was extremely important even if there were no purchases to make. Here's how much it meant. At about the age of ten, I went to the hospital to have my tonsils removed. I was discharged after a day or so, with instructions to eat lots of soups and liquids. Mom saw to it that I had what I needed to eat, and I recuperated for several days. But when Saturday arrived and it was time to go to town, I was still not back to health.

Mom decided that she was going to town nonetheless, which meant that I was going too. It was a hot summer and businesses did not have air conditioning; they only had ceiling fans, which didn't do much good. Mom seemed to stop in every store, and I tagged along. While she was talking with someone in one of the stores, I tried to get her attention to tell her I was not feeling well. Naturally, she brushed me off as a tiresome little boy bothering his mom while she talked with her friend.

After two or three tries at getting Mom's attention, the last thing I remember was reaching for the front of her dress. I awoke minutes later to find myself in the arms of a man I did not know and had never seen before. He was kind and helpful enough to carry me out of the hot store onto the street for some fresher air. He continued carrying me to our car parked a bit away. From that day forward, Mom promised to make sure that I was well before worrying about going to town or anywhere else.

It seemed that something was always happening to me—nothing catastrophic, just annoying. For example, one day when I was about eleven or twelve years old, I was playing on our front porch near the highway. I decided to run through the front door into the house. My right ankle struck a protruding nail end that ripped my ankle wide open. As I realized what had happened, I sat on the floor and looked at the whiteness of the inner part of my ankle as it slowly began to bleed. I was scared to death and screamed at my mom to come to see about me. She wrapped my wound as best she could with cloth.

There was no effort to take me to a doctor or to treat the injury with anything other than homemade remedies. In our community, our parents all thought that castor oil and Vicks VapoRub could cure anything and everything. There was nothing I hated more than castor oil. I often thought to myself, "How could something that tastes so bad cure anyone?" Not seeing a doctor proved okay for a few days, but left me with a very sore and swollen ankle.

My dad had taken up arranging bus trips to Atlantic Beach, the Black visitors' beach in South Carolina, just a short distance from Myrtle Beach, the destination for white visitors. Black people could not go to Myrtle Beach in 1950s segregated South Carolina, so it was Atlantic Beach or no beach. Dad charged passengers a fee and sold water to supplement what he collected. Such trips usually occurred once a year and were a joyous time for the farm-based residents.

On one Sunday morning, about a week after injuring my ankle, we prepared to embark on one of my dad's bus trips to the beach. But before I could leave, I had to tend to the cow. She stepped on my injured ankle and busted it open again. I cried, but I did not miss the bus to the beach. Once I was at the beach, playing in the saltwater, my wound was thoroughly cleansed, the pain went away, and I forgot about it for the rest of the day. When I returned home, healing commenced almost immediately, and that ankle never bothered me again. So once again, nature was our doctor. Mom and Dad could not have been happier that they did not have to worry about me and my ankle anymore.

This community bus trip to Atlantic Beach was probably my most memorable. Aside from the curing of my ankle wound, I experienced a fright generated by a blowout on the right front tire of the bus while we were traveling at about sixty miles per hour. That blowout caused the bus to pull hard to the right side of the highway, which was bordered by a deep gorge. I was sitting up front on the right side of the bus and envisioned the bus tumbling into the gorge. The bus driver reacted quickly and turned the steering wheel as far left as possible, holding it steady while applying the brakes as hard as he could. The bus came to a stop just at the edge of the gorge. I am sure there were many prayers among the passengers that morning and grateful cries of "thank you, Lordy" when the bus finally reached a safe stop. That incident put a damper on the remainder of the ride to the beach. But once there, I forgot about it, enjoying the water, sunshine, food, drinks, and camaraderie.

That was my second close brush with death or serious injury. My first one occurred at about age eleven or twelve. Several of us boys were waiting for our mothers, who were attending a meeting at Elizabeth Baptist Church. We talked and played outside the church and decided to visit the corner grocery store a few hundred feet away. As we approached the store entrance, a drunken white man between twenty-five and thirty-five years old came out. Without provocation of any kind, he suddenly pulled out a large pistol and pointed it directly at my head. He was less than three or four feet from me. I slowly backed away as he ranted incoherently, threatening to shoot all of us. I thought I might die that evening. Only later did I realize my death would have been for no other reason than that I was a Black boy and he was a drunk white adult.

After we all backed away, he finally left us alone and went on his way. We never told the storeowner about the incident, but we did tell our parents. But they had no avenue to complain about a white man terrorizing little Black boys, so there was no consequence of any kind. That experience stayed with me, and I imagine, with the others as well, for quite some time. I remember it vividly even today.

When I was fifteen, my father informed us that we would no longer engage in farming and that we were moving to Florence, South Carolina, to live in the new house that we had worked hard to build over the past couple of years. I was very pleased. A year earlier, I'd spent time in Florence with my aunt and uncle, Bazella and Booker T. King, and attended middle school with their son, Booker T. King, Jr. For the first time, I had a play and study partner.

In high school in Florence, I was quiet, studied hard, played the clarinet in the school band, and had a singing part in the school choir during one Christmas concert. I enjoyed being in the band and the particular pleasure of our annual trek—for about three consecutive years—to participate in the Cherry Blossom Parade in Washington, D.C. The parades were long and demanding; however, we loved the crowd recognition as we marched along. During these trips, we also had the opportunity to visit and stay at several Historically Black Colleges and Universities (HBCUs), including Hampton Institute, now Hampton University, in Hampton, Virginia.

During one of those trips, several of us boys decided to visit the Washington Monument and walk from the ground floor to the top. What a mistake. By the time we had climbed hundreds of stairs and finally reached the top, we were so hot and sweaty and worn out that we had stripped our clothes down to the waist. Most of us were determined to ride the elevator back to ground level, and we promised ourselves that we would not try that again.

Another evening, we decided to leave our hotel and take in some of the Washington, D.C., sights. Our chaperones warned us that it was dangerous to be out alone and said that we should stay together in a group and be very vigilant about our surroundings. I decided to take along one of the majorettes' batons for protection.

We encountered two police officers who wanted to know who we were and what we were doing out on the street. They immediately focused on me and my baton, wanting to know why I was carrying a metal stick. When they asked what it was, I explained that it was a baton, but the cops did not understand (or pretended not to understand) and acted as though it was a weapon. Finally, one of the boys in our group realized the problem and told the cops that I was holding a majorette twirling stick from our band and that we were in town to march in the parade. They calmed down, told us to be careful, and said that I could keep the baton. I am not sure why the police were so interested in the baton, except that it was being carried in a group of young Black men walking down the street together. Not much has changed even today.

In 1953, at the age of sixteen, I applied for and received a South Carolina school bus driver's certificate and drove a regular school bus route for the 1953–1954 school year. The state needed bus drivers in Florence County and the man in charge of drivers was happy to have me. As a high school junior, this made me feel important, and some of the student riders looked upon me as someone special. Plus, I earned money as a driver, which served as a source of support when I attended college later. Driving the bus also gave me a bit of status with some of the girls at school. One girl who rode my bus caught my interest, and we had a relationship for one year. When I no longer drove the bus, I decided that she lived too far for me to continue seeing her.

My main girlfriend was Luvenia Jackson, who lived on the north side of Florence. We were a regular item at Wilson High School and in town. I remember how eager I was to hear from her when she went away to visit relatives one summer. It seemed as if it took her forever to write me, and I had no means of contacting her. It wasn't as long as it appeared—but I thought so, because I was in love. She went to college in South Carolina, and I went to Georgia, and we grew apart. I discovered that she had another boyfriend at school, which ended our relationship. Although I never heard from or saw her again, I will never forget her.

Before becoming a school bus driver, I walked into one of the most popular restaurants in Florence County to ask for a job. The clientele was 100 percent white. The manager queried me about my experience as a waiter, and I had to admit I had none. I told him I learned fast. Something convinced him that I could do the job, and he hired me to work beside grown men who had families to support. I received the same pay they did. Surprisingly, I was well liked by some of the patrons. Sometimes they would request that I serve them. I often marveled to myself that with my salary and tips, I was making as much money a week as my dad, who was working extremely hard, full-time, and had a family to support.

Unfortunately, some people working with me at the restaurant envied my status. One of them set me up negatively in front of the manager, who felt it necessary to fire me. The incident was bizarre. On a somewhat slow evening, with few patrons in the restaurant, I visited in the kitchen with the short-order head cook—whom I considered a friend—between trips checking on my table.

He said to me, "Look, this piece of pie is unfit for serving to customers, so why don't you eat it?"

Thinking nothing of the offer, since he was the head cook, I took the pie and began nibbling on it between trips to check on my one table. The manager saw me taking bites here and there and confronted me. I told him exactly what the cook had told me. Nonetheless, he accused me of stealing it. I tried unsuccessfully to explain to him that I had no reason to steal a twenty-cent piece of pie when I had money in my pocket from my tips and wages. I offered to pay for the piece of pie, but the manager was having none of it. The head cook stood there and said not a word.

To this day, I believe that had the cook simply said, "I told Press to eat the pie because it's not fit to serve to customers," I would have never been fired. I learned a valuable lesson that day about people who pretend to be your friend. Perhaps my fellow worker felt that I was simply too young or too big for my britches. After this setback, I turned my attention toward attending college. In fact, I was more determined than ever to do so.

When our family moved to the southeastern section of Florence, my dad secured a job working at an outdoor plant nursery. In addition to his work at the nursery, he also spent a great deal of time as a long-distance driver between Georgia, Florida, and Florence, handling the plants and accessories. The job was okay; however, it subjected Dad to almost constant wet conditions. He often had a cold or related condition, although he rarely allowed sickness to keep him from work. Still, I feared that eventually he would develop something severe. I wanted him to find another job, away from the wet environment.

Shortly before I graduated from Wilson High School, I learned the principal was seeking a new janitor. Hearing this, I went to him and asked him to consider my dad for the job. I can't remember whether I ever told Dad that I recommended him to the principal. Dad landed the job, which relieved my concern that he might contract pneumonia working in the wet environment of the nursery. I don't know why the principal listened to me, but I was extremely thankful he did. I graduated before Dad started work at Wilson High. He started that position in 1955 and retired with an excess of twenty-five years of service. He received retirement benefits as well.

My high school days were mainly joyous. I did not have a lot of friends, and I did not seek to be part of ongoing recreational or sports activities, but my classmates and other school personnel liked me. I earned good grades, had strong support from my parents, and even had a girlfriend or two. My girlfriends' mothers liked me, which gave me a leg up on the competition. They would often tell their daughters what a good boy and how well behaved I was.

When I was in ninth grade, a new family from Georgia moved into town and their son enrolled in the high school. The Bells were a family of four: father, mother, daughter, and son. It did not take long for the son, Fred Bell Jr., and I to become friends, and soon very close friends. We spent most of our time together. We were members of the Boy Scouts, and we went back and forth to each other's homes. We were proud of ourselves for not getting into trouble. No one said bad things about us.

Nonetheless, we sometimes made terrible decisions. Once we were walking to school and encountered two large dogs behind a fence that ran parallel to the street. Because the dogs were fenced in and viciously barking at us, we decided to agitate them. As we walked along, teasing the dogs, the fence suddenly ended, and the dogs were free. I don't believe we ever ran so fast in our lives. Luckily, the dogs chose not to follow us very far, and we breathed a welcome sigh of relief about two blocks later. You can bet that we promised ourselves never to do anything like that again. Years later, Fred and I laughed about that encounter—but there was no laughter the day it happened.

A beloved teacher confessed to us that his big dream was to own a Cadillac. He was proud that he had just purchased a brand-new 1955 Chevrolet. He saw that car as a stepping stone to satisfying his big dream. Mindful of his confession, Fred and I focused on attending college. It's possible that episode was responsible for me declaring that I never wanted to own a Cadillac. I thought owning a Cadillac was for the bourgeoisie, which I was determined not to be.

CHAPTER 3

Going to College

Fred and I were both admitted to Morehouse College, "the House," in Atlanta, Georgia. This was the school attended by Dr. Martin Luther King Jr., both his sons, his brother, his father, and his grandfather. Many people considered Morehouse the only college on the planet for Black men. Dr. King was admitted to Morehouse in 1944, eleven years before me, and graduated in 1948. He became a legend at the school. The average Morehouse student at the time, however, including myself, did not fully grasp King's involvement in the civil rights movement or the scope of his national stature.

Fred was an early admittance student to Morehouse, entering after the eleventh grade, but I decided to complete high school before enrolling in college. I thought finishing high school would better prepare me, and also that I needed all the education and money I could get before tackling college. I kept remembering Dad's words, which he said to me more than once: "If you want to go to college, I will find a way to make it happen." I knew my parents didn't have any money, yet I believed in him so much that I had faith that it would come to fruition.

Thus, after graduating from Wilson High School in 1955, I enrolled at Morehouse College under the presidency of Dr. Benjamin Elijah Mays. My dad wanted me to attend Claflin College, now Claflin University, in Orangeburg, South Carolina. I was not surprised that he wanted me to attend Claflin, since he was a devout Methodist and Claflin is an affiliate of the United Methodist Church. I did not want to attend Claflin and chose Morehouse instead. Dad gave me no opposition when I told him of my decision. I received a full-tuition scholarship to Morehouse of $275. Yet this did not cover the full cost of attending for the school year 1955–56.

I was the first member of my close family to attend college; it was not something that many in my community aspired to do. I did briefly consider attending a majority-white school, such as Kent State in Ohio, but in the end I had no thought about attending anything other than an HBCU—and certainly not one of the white South Carolina schools.

HBCUs are majority-Black institutions founded before 1964. There are considerable discussions about the need for such schools, now that white institutions are available to Blacks. I believe HBCUs are needed as much now as ever before. They have a joint unique mission: to provide support for minority students and to motivate them to seek their full potential. These schools are very much alive, diverse (public research, elite liberal arts, religious, and secular), and they address the needs of many minority students. Even today, many students attending an HBCU are the first in their families to attend college. HBCUs have been training such students for many years and have the know-how to do so effectively.

I had little knowledge of Dr. Mays and Morehouse College before my enrollment. I followed my best friend to "the House" because Fred was from Georgia and knew all about the school and its reputation. It did not take me long to learn about the dynamic Dr. Mays's Baptist ministry and civil rights background, and Morehouse's eighty-eight years as a "Builder of Men." Dr. Mays received credit for laying the intellectual foundations of this country's civil rights movement and for Morehouse never failing to contribute her share to the fostering of humanity through a "culture for service" amidst the political emancipation of the Black race.

Dr. Mays was a tremendously well-respected and nationally recognized educator and civil rights activist. He was also a dynamic speaker. He famously said, "It must be borne in mind that the tragedy of life does not lie in not reaching your goal. The tragedy of life lies in having no goal to reach."

Dr. Mays was also a man with a caring heart, as I had personal reason to know. In the middle of my sophomore year I found myself out of money, facing the possibility of having to leave school. Knowing that my family could not help, I told Dr. Mays about my situation and asked if he could help. He said, "Let me think about it, and I will let you know."

Dr. Mays found sufficient funds to enable me to complete that year at Morehouse. Fortunately, I was able to combine other Morehouse scholarships and monies earned during the school year and summer work to adequately cover my college expenses for the remaining two years. I owe an enormous debt of gratitude to my half-sister, Ruthie Lee, and my paternal cousin Lonnie Harrison, both of Brooklyn, New York; my maternal uncle, Malikiah "Mallie" Isaiah, of Long Island; and their families for accepting me and providing a home for me during those summer work stints.

As a freshman at Morehouse, I was initially a bit homesick as I had never been away from home for any length of time. That feeling soon passed away as I buckled down and got serious about college. I knew that things would be tough when we spent the first week at school taking various tests to determine our class placements. I worried I might be less prepared than other first-year students and wondered if I could keep up. I did well on the tests, though, and between that testing period and my early class performance, I concluded that I could compete with almost any of the students around me, even if I had to spend more time studying and working than most of them.

According to the school doctor, Dr. James B. Ellison, I took things much too seriously at first, as evidenced by my constant complaints to him of recurring stomachaches. His advice to me was to stop worrying about everything or I would develop an ulcer. Slowly but surely, the stomachaches disappeared as I tried to heed his advice and also gained more confidence in my abilities to succeed.

Despite Fred enrolling a year before I did, we both graduated from Morehouse with bachelor's degrees in May 1959. Fred's degree was in biology, and mine was in chemistry. I think both of us had early aspirations of becoming medical doctors. Because my instructors and advisers at Morehouse emphasized that medical schools preferred students who were well-rounded educationally (thus trained in a field other than or in addition to biology) and preferred to teach biological subjects to the medical students themselves, I chose chemistry as my area of preparation. In the end, however, neither Fred nor I went into medicine. I remember confessing to myself and anyone who would listen that I certainly did not want potential patients calling me for a home visit at 3 a.m. (Doctors made house calls routinely in those days.) With his degree in biology, Fred became a high-level administrator in the government medical world.

My first-year class in chemistry consisted of about three hundred students. I remember our teacher, Dr. Henry C. McBay, commenting during our first class meeting that the size of our class would decrease by half in the first year and would continue to decrease until graduation. Dr. McBay, a legend in his own right, taught many of the nation's leading Black scientists, dentists, and physicians. His words were prophetic: half of the three hundred students either failed or dropped the class after midterms. By graduation, there were only four of us left.

I cannot say that I have second-guessed my time spent studying and in the chemistry laboratories, which kept me from joining my friends in sitting out on the lawn, courting girls, and visiting them when allowed by their schools. Morehouse was an all-boys school in very close proximity to the co-ed Clark College and the all-girls Spelman College; we were also not very far away from another co-ed learning center, Morris Brown College. Those schools were all part of the Atlanta University Center, a graduate-level institution.

Despite the temptation, I was determined to stay the course and perform well academically, which often meant observing boys and girls having fun on the lawn, holding hands, or walking through campus while I was busy in the chemistry laboratory. I routinely took 17–19 credit hours each semester beginning in September 1955 and ending in May 1959. The label I earned in high school, "bookworm," stayed with me through college. I didn't let the title bother me. I had to study much more than the other students, but I was determined to be a good scholar.

A side benefit to working during the summers was that it gave me opportunities to visit, live and work in, and enjoy the city of New York and its riches. Living with Lonnie's family provided me with the experience of residing in a row house. To my amazement, I quickly learned to distinguish our building from the other nearly identical row houses. Like many other subway riders, I learned how to sleep on the subway and wake up just in time to get off at my designated stop. The young women who lived in the area were not bad either: I found a girlfriend who lived in the same building as I did. In the end, though, I didn't bother to partake of the vast social life of the town in a big way. I tolerated the borough of Brooklyn for two summers; I loved living in Queens.

My first summer in New York, in 1955, found me working with Uncle Mallie building homes. My jobs consisted of securing materials, driving a truck, installing insulation, and digging sewer-pipe trenches between the buildings under construction. My first day on the job was going reasonably well until I became overheated while digging pipe trenches and fainted (it was hot out there). I was alone when this occurred, and no one saw me or knew of my predicament. I did manage to make it inside one of the houses under construction before fainting, which put me on the ground in the shade. I came to after a few minutes with the worst headache since my pre-eyeglass-wearing days.

When I informed my uncle, he immediately proceeded to cut my rather large "bush" hairstyle and put me to bed. I slept for hours, wakened, and slowly returned to normal. But that was enough for my uncle. He found me a different job, helping to deliver beer to New York businesses. He didn't say so, but I suspect he concluded that as a college boy I had grown soft and was nothing like the farm boy I used to be.

The work assignment was much better than digging trenches, but given that I weighed at most 135 pounds, I struggled to handle a dolly loaded with beer up and down steps, in and out of basements. I also had the challenging task of meeting the owner/driver of the delivery truck at a different part of the city each morning, which was difficult since I knew little about using the subway system.

A significant part of my job was to prevent people from stealing beer off the truck while the owner/driver was making deliveries. I would stand by the truck with a stick or rod in hand, watching each side and chasing would-be thieves away. No matter how hard I tried, sometimes a few beers disappeared. I must confess that I was glad when that summer ended and I could return to Morehouse for the academic year.

For some reason, Uncle Mallie allowed me to drive his automobile in regular traffic but refused that right to his son, Eugene, who was about seven months younger than me. That made Gene angry with both of us, though it did not change the situation. Uncle Mallie told Gene that he was too irresponsible and wild to drive a car. Thereafter Gene was not always kind to me since he felt I was being treated better than he was. I imagine he was glad to see me leave.

I blame my aversion to writing letters for my loss of contact with Uncle Mallie and his family, but I never forgot them. My Ancestry journey revealed that Gene married Alma Salters in 1963 or so. They had one son, and Gene died in 1995.

During the summer of 1956, I accepted a job as a domestic for a white Boy Scouts camp far from my home in Florence. It was a beautiful camp located deep in the woods, and there were many activities for the attendees, none of which I could participate in. Back then, I could not swim; I never really had an opportunity to learn how until I went to that camp. At night, following the completion of my chores, I quietly slipped down to the swimming dock. I would slowly venture out into the water and swim back to the pier, increasing my distance as I felt comfortable. There was no one at the camp that I could tell I could not swim and wanted to learn how. There was no one to ask for help. But after that summer experience, I was no longer terrified of the water.

I don't know if any of my friends knew how to swim. There were no ready and safe swimming holes that we were aware of. Our parents and other adults constantly admonished us to stay away from any water bodies we came across, usually waterholes. There was so much that we did not have access to or did not know about—a common theme throughout much of my life. Much later in life, I finally learned to be semi-comfortable in deep water because of the tutelage of Coach Louis Hightower, a physical education teacher at Southern University. In his spare time one semester, Coach Hightower taught me and other Southern faculty and staff how to swim. I was the lone male in the group.

In 1957, my second summer in New York City, I worked for General Linen, Inc. I have little memory of that job, probably because I did not like it very much. But it served its purpose, as I earned money for school. I needed a place to stay, so Mom reached out to Ruthie Lee and Eddie, and they accepted me with open arms. It was great seeing Ruthie Lee again after such a long time. I also got the chance to meet their daughter Margie, who was between one and two years old and still crawling.

Margie was such a joy. She would wait by the front door every day until I returned from work. She knew just when I should be home and coming through the door. We would have playtime for fifteen to twenty minutes, and then she was off to something else. I never figured out what it was about me that made her become so attached. Ruthie Lee had no problems leaving Margie with me as a babysitter. Eddie worked at a bakery, a job with odd hours, so I didn't see much of him most of the summer. Ruthie Lee was on maternity leave and spent much time working to lose the baby fat she had gained during her pregnancy with Margie.

Once I returned to Morehouse College, we lost touch again and I didn't meet their other children, Lynn and Edith, until they were teenagers. By then, Ruthie Lee and Eddie had moved back to Florence and had built a home a short distance down the street from our house, where my dad lived alone in his retirement. Their attention to my dad in the years before he died made me overlook the dispute Ruthie Lee and I had about paying for his funeral. All in all, she was a good half-sister, and Eddie was an excellent half-brother-in-law.

In 1958, during my third summer in New York, I landed a job with a postal stamp machine manufacturing firm owned by a man named George Wartell, who expected his workers to be on time and to work every minute of the day except during their morning and afternoon breaks. My initial assignment was relatively routine. Soon it morphed into shipping all machines to various destinations worldwide. It was a specialty job, and I was responsible for fulfilling the entire order correctly as to the type of machine, the number of devices, accessories, and shipping address, in addition to the machine parts that I fabricated. I found that job particularly rewarding, including the experience of mailing materials worldwide.

At least a couple of young ladies working there found me attractive enough to let me date them, which added considerable joy to my summer. However, they were not my only attractions. I must admit that my social life was pretty good considering that I was a stranger in town.

I very seldom made enough money during those summer periods to cover my school costs, so I also sought employment during the regular school year. The first job that I secured was as a busboy and dishwasher at an Italian restaurant in Atlanta. My duties were to keep the tables, dishes, and silverware clean and available for use by customers. The restaurant hours were usually 5:30 p.m. to 10:30 p.m., which meant I would finish cleaning up about midnight. The job was tremendously difficult since I had 8 a.m. classes most days of the week. Trying to carry on with such a deficit in sleep did not bode well for my academic success.

I kept that job for several months while looking for something more compatible with my study and class schedules. Success came my way when I landed a job at Wang's Camera Shop. The shop occupied a prominent place on Peachtree Street in the heart of the commercial district. Wang's sold cameras, televisions, radios, and other personal use equipment.

My job consisted of delivering items purchased by buyers that were too large for them to take home themselves. When there were no deliveries, I made sure that the beautiful glass shelves in the store were free of dust and fingerprints. Atlanta's traffic was horrific, and it often took hours for me to deliver one item depending on where in the city or suburbs the buyer lived. The length of my delivery trip also depended on whether or not I had to set up the equipment. I had no previous experience setting up such items (nearly all TVs), but I did a creditable job, even on my first time out.

Jim Crow law ruled the day in 1950s Georgia, a fact of which I was well aware as I made my Wang's deliveries to white customers. One particular delivery bothered me tremendously. A rather attractive young white woman purchased a television at Wang's that required delivery and setup. When I arrived at her home and began setting up the TV, I noticed she was friendly and talkative, which surprised me. Running through my mind was just how close she might get and then pretend that I was the aggressor. I made sure that I did not respond to any of her gestures, got the TV up and running, and hurriedly vacated the premises.

I liked the job at Wang's because it was clean, my work hours ended no later than 6:30 p.m., and most of my deliveries were on Saturdays. The store management was pleasant and appeared to like me, but more importantly, they appreciated my status as a college student. I worked at Wang's until I graduated. My graduation present was an excellent Yashica A camera, which became my prized possession and served me well at Howard University.

Lots of work or not, I found some time to devote to girls. I briefly dated a lovely young lady attending Spelman College. Our relationship was cut short because I discovered that she was only fifteen years old, while I was eighteen. That did not seem right to me, and I felt as if I were robbing the cradle. About a year later, I met another sweet young lady who attended Clark College. I was more adept at managing my study and class workloads and found enough time to spend with her to make the relationship enjoyable. She invited me to her hometown of Milledgeville, Georgia, to meet her parents. I reluctantly agreed and spent several days at her parents' home during a Christmas holiday break. It was fun traveling with her by bus to her hometown and spending those days at her parents' house. The house was out in the country, a good distance from town; there was not much to do and few places to go. Her parents treated me very well and made me feel special.

The only part of that visit I found distasteful was the bus ride from Milledgeville to my hometown of Florence. Seemingly, that was the longest bus ride I ever had. The one-way trip seemed to take forever. We stopped at every little town, sometimes for hours at a time. I had to get food from the back door of the bus stations and use the "colored" restrooms, if there were any. I liked this girl a lot, but I was determined not to repeat that experience. Thus, I never visited her home again, and we lost contact when I graduated from Morehouse.

One activity I remember well from my college days was eating at the dining hall. The cafeteria food was wholesome enough. The problem was that the menu rarely changed from week to week. Like every other school I visited or heard students talk about, the food was okay but not great.

Assemblies, however, were exciting. We got to listen to some wonderful speakers. Students were required to attend assemblies, and roll was called each time. Each student had an assigned seat in the auditorium, and the roll taker only had to look to see which seats were vacant to know who was absent. Academic Dean Brailsford Brazeal and others made a point of reminding us that assembly attendance was mandatory, as was our best-dressed attire, which meant I had to wear a suit and tie. The Morehouse Glee Club would occasionally entertain us. We were proud of the Glee Club. They performed all over America.

Majoring in chemistry and minoring in mathematics meant that I spent a lot of time with the professors in those subjects. I particularly remember chemistry professor Dr. Henry C. McBay and math professor Claude B. "Pop" Dansby. Both set high standards for my college performance.

Other Morehouse faculty members of whom I have fond memories were Dellie L. Boger, Ed.D. (Psychology & Education); Robert H. Brisbane Jr., Ph.D. (Political Science); Sabinus H. Christenson, Ph.D. (Physics); Edward A. Jones, Ph.D. (Foreign Language); Wendell P. Whalum, A.M. (Music); and Samuel W. Williams, B.D. and A.M. (Philosophy & Religion).

Upperclassmen warned me not to take Dr. Christenson's physics class because "he took no prisoners." Most students before me failed his class, as did most of those who took it with me. Dr. Christenson was tough but also fair, and he stood ready to provide any help one needed. I took full advantage of his generosity, learned his testing methodologies and quirks, and earned A's and B's throughout the course. Dr. Christenson liked giving exams and flipping a problem given earlier upside-down at a subsequent testing. Many students never caught on to his trick and continually failed their tests.

My favorite teacher was Dr. McBay, my primary chemistry instructor. He was not very talkative, though he said enough for you to know where he stood on issues. He had one strange behavior—always walking ahead of his wife when they were together. Students didn't know what to make of that situation and dared not ask him.

Dr. Boger was a special connection because he was from my hometown of Florence and provided my transportation to and from home during the holidays and at the end of the school year. I constantly wondered how he managed to fit all the suitcases in the trunk of his car when carrying his wife, two other students, and me. Even though the distance from Atlanta to Florence is only 321 miles, the trip seemed to take forever since those were the days before interstate highways.

Without Dr. Boger's generosity, I would have had no way of going home during college, since money was scarce. He never charged us a penny for his help. We did, as best we could, supply some money for gasoline.

Like all freshmen at Morehouse, I lived in Graves Hall for my first year of college. Then I moved to a group of dormitories referred to as "the Units." My room was Unit 5, room 106, which was on the first floor. I had two roommates, William T. Barnes and Wiley Perdue. Both were upperclassmen and Alpha Phi Alpha fraternity members. They were as fine roommates as anyone could wish to have, and they treated me as their friend. Yet what I witnessed in their treatment of fraternity pledges convinced me that I wanted no part in being one, Alpha or otherwise. I had no intention of putting up with such utter nonsense that I saw pledges do.

I played the clarinet in the band for the first two years of college and thoroughly enjoyed it. However, it interfered with my studies and class performance, so I reluctantly resigned at the beginning of my junior year. Mr. Whalum, the band director, expressed sorrow at my decision, but he understood that academics came before anything else at Morehouse. That was the last time I played the clarinet in an organized fashion for a sustained period.

Life is a paradox, and one never knows what it will bring. In my youth, I decided that I did not like politics and never wanted to be a part of it. I considered it nasty and sometimes downright disgusting. Also, I disavowed ever wanting to be a teacher or owning a Cadillac. Nonetheless, over the course of my life, I found myself doing all three.

While at Morehouse in 1957, several other students and I became interested in the ambitious effort of Theodore Martin Alexander Sr. to become the first elected Black city alderman in Atlanta. Mr. Alexander recognized the absence of Black representation in electoral politics in both the city of Atlanta and the state of Georgia for more than ninety years. Thus, he embarked on an effort to become the first Black Georgia state senator in 1961.

Although unsuccessful in each of his bids, his actions motivated other Black candidates to seek election to public office, thus paving the foundation for the first Black person elected mayor of the City of Atlanta and for numerous other Black officials throughout the South.

Those of us who participated in Mr. Alexander's runs for elective office had a tremendous opportunity, even though I did not realize the impact it would have on my life. That foray into the political arena and my NAACP involvement set the stage, unknowingly, for my political efforts, some of which qualify as firsts.

Recalling my involvement in Mr. Alexander's campaigns reminds me of my efforts to register to vote for the first time in Florence. I had reached the age of twenty-one (the minimum voting age at the time) by August 1957 after my sophomore year at Morehouse, and I wanted to register to vote at the local courthouse. I took my mother with me, and I told the white female clerk why I was there. After carefully looking me over, she told me to read and interpret the U.S. Constitution to her.

I had already told her that I had completed my sophomore year at Morehouse College, but that did not impress her. She insisted that I read and interpret the Constitution. Insulted as I was, I knew my goal was to be registered to vote, no matter what it took to do so. I took the copy of the Constitution and read the first two lines. She stopped me and said, "That's okay. Sign right here."

I can only assume my ability to read and pronounce every word correctly convinced her that not only was I literate, but also that I might challenge her if she denied me the opportunity to register. I quietly signed the registration card and then told her in a determined tone that I wanted my mother to register as well. She did not argue with me and proceeded to register my mother without any pushback. That day in Florence, South Carolina, two Black persons registered to vote without suffering the fate of Otis Moss Sr., who went to three different places in rural Georgia in 1946 in an attempt to vote for the first time.

Officials at the first two places told Mr. Moss that he was at the wrong place. At the third location, he was told he was too late and the office had closed. Otis Moss Sr. walked eighteen miles that day but did not achieve his goal to vote. South Carolina was pretty much like that in 1957, though we did not have to trudge eighteen miles with no concrete result.

Today, the methods of minority voter suppression may have changed, but the effects are the same as they were in 1957. Many younger minority folks do not think there is a need to continue to fight today.

Despite the passage of the Voting Rights Act in 1965, minority voters today are still subjected to discriminatory voting policies implemented by state and local officials throughout the United States. Some politicians are determined to create and keep in place multiple obstacles to Black voters' full political participation. State and local officials consistently have drawn electoral maps that restrict the ability of Black voters to participate in elections on equal footing with white voters. Many Black voters also lack equal access to polling sites and early voting locations and are thwarted by efforts to reduce voting by mail.

Election officials dilute Black voting strength by "packing" (concentrating large Black voting-age populations into fewer districts than required by demographics) and "cracking" (dispersing one voting bloc across many districts). Packing and cracking are electoral gerrymandering tools widely used by state and local officials.

Other restrictive measures include a prohibition on distributing water to voters while they wait in line; voter intimidation; and using a narrow definition of "Black," under which citizens who identify themselves to the census as both Black and another race or ethnicity would not be counted as Black. At-large elections in which minority voters are outnumbered due to the large physical area included in the district and inequitable felony disenfranchisement rules also restrict Black voting strength.

I strongly encourage every Black person of voting age to commit to doing the following:

1. Register to vote.
2. Vote in every election; every vote does count.
3. Bring your children with you to the polls and show them how to push the buttons on the machines.
4. Encourage your family members and friends to vote in every election.
5. Hold your elected representatives accountable.

In May 1959, I graduated from Morehouse College with a major in chemistry and a minor in mathematics. My final grade point average was 3.2, which was enough to earn me graduation with honors—one of less than ten honor graduates in our class—and a graduate assistantship at Howard University in Washington, D.C. Unfortunately, neither my mom nor dad could attend the graduation ceremonies. They had no money to travel. That hurt my mom a lot, and me too, since she was the primary motivator for me to attend college.

After spending the summer at home in Florence with my parents, I was off to Howard, seeking a master's degree in chemistry. The dollar amount of my teaching assistantship provided little more than tuition ($13 per credit hour) and room and board, and it took more than a month for the university to begin paying the stipend.

Sad to say, I had to live off of extremely meager funds that first month and found myself eating a hamburger, fries, and a cherry coke most days for lunch. Sometimes I only had one meal a day. I lost quite a bit of weight and could not afford to do so, as I then weighed only 125–130 pounds when properly fed. Once payments began, however, things looked up. I spent my first year living in off-campus university housing about one mile from campus.

As was the case when I attended Morehouse, I enjoyed an excellent relationship with my roommate. We spent practically all of our non-class time together except when he was courting girls. On one of our 1959 outings to downtown Washington, we noticed many people gathering in and about the area near the White House. Inquiring as to what was happening, we learned that President Dwight D. Eisenhower and General Secretary Nikita Khrushchev might arrive soon. We decided to wait and see the president and Mr. Khrushchev, since the meeting was so historic. We waited for hours, and when they finally did arrive, they rushed into the White House so quickly that we barely knew they had come. Needless to say, we were very disappointed. A year later, Mr. Khrushchev notoriously brought attention to himself by banging his shoe on a podium at the United Nations.

After that first year, my roommate's and my paths separated, as we were in different academic disciplines. I moved from the university dormitory to the Alpha Phi Alpha fraternity house on New Hampshire Avenue. Even though the distance to campus was farther than it was from the dormitory, the daily walks back and forth were not bad. On April 9, 1960, I became a member of the Omicron Lambda Alpha chapter of the fraternity in Washington, D.C., a step I was unwilling to take at Morehouse. But the members of the Omicron chapter (an intermediate chapter between undergraduate and graduate) were college graduates and career men, and they had neither time nor interest in the silly behavior in which undergraduates tended to engage. That suited me just fine. Living at the fraternity house was cheaper than living in the university dormitory, and I had full access to all the common areas of the house, including the kitchen. That is where I learned to cook, for if you didn't cook your meals you didn't eat.

As part of our pledging requirements, we had to learn about outstanding Alpha men like the Seven Jewels (founders), as well as Thurgood Marshall, Belford Lawson, and Martin Luther King Jr. It was especially fascinating to learn about attorney Lawson. He was a recent president of Alpha Phi Alpha and was the first Black attorney to win a case before the Supreme Court. He lived in Washington, D.C., in the 1960s, and I was fortunate to meet him in person. Lawson was that shining example of a man with his finger on the pulse of Black America and a model for what we could achieve.

All was not peaches and cream at the fraternity house. One of my fraternity brothers took the liberty of entering my room, rummaging through my belongings, and stealing my prized Yashica A camera, along with some cash. I reported the theft to the authorities, who identified the person responsible and arrested him.

The thief turned out to be one of the brothers closest to me. After I confronted him and he denied having taken the items, I tried to have the case dismissed, but the district attorney would have none of it. I lost contact with that brother following his conviction, and I believe he went to jail. Once again, I'd experienced in a stark fashion that someone who seems to be your friend is not necessarily what he appears to be.

I must admit that experience caused me to develop a bitter attitude about living in the fraternity house and the security of my possessions. As I recall, the rooms did not have locks. I thus joined forces with two other men and we rented an apartment together, which elevated our living status quite a bit. The distance to campus was about the same as it was from the fraternity house. We remained in that location for a year or so. I was then fortunate enough to occupy a house in a well-respected neighborhood on the northeast side of D.C. My best friend from high school, Fred Bell, was my roommate.

Fred worked for the federal government in the health sciences field and became a well-respected and high-ranking administrator. Meanwhile, I completed my assistantship, earning a master's degree in physical chemistry and a minor in organic chemistry under the guidance of Dr. J. L. Shereshefshy. Fred and I remained friends throughout the years until his untimely death in 2012. I thought he was a picture of health, but he died of a massive heart attack.

Howard had lots of pretty female students, though I did not have the opportunity to get acquainted with many of them. There were very few female students in the graduate chemistry program. The chemistry department was self-contained, housing all of its classes in one building. It even had its own library. There was little reason for me to visit other parts of the campus, except occasionally to use the main library.

It was assumed back then that most women attended Howard with the express purpose of landing a doctor or lawyer as a husband. Therefore, the coeds seemed to prefer the medical and law students. That was probably for the best, since I didn't have a chance for much interaction with them and they probably had no time for a lowly chemistry major like me.

I did date one undergraduate, Patricia, from Columbia, South Carolina. I visited her once in Columbia and met her wonderful family. Once I graduated and began teaching at Southern University in Baton Rouge, Louisiana, I lost contact with Patricia, who was still a student at Howard. There were many good-looking women at Southern and in Baton Rouge, which made it easy to forget Washington, Howard, and all that went with them, including Patricia.

During my last two years at Howard, I spent a lot of time with my good friend Tommie, who worked at the National Institutes of Health and was a native Washingtonian. He, too, had a difficult time meeting young ladies. We spent a lot of time looking, especially on the dance floor. Tommie was a superb and smooth dancer and taught me many of his dance moves. I dated some lovely girls, yet none really caught my fancy.

One of these girls invited me to visit her at her home in Maryland. I took the bus from near my house to hers. She neglected to inform me, however, that the bus only ran until 9 p.m. Not knowing that, I stayed with her until 10 p.m., when the bus was no longer running its route. She made no effort to assist me in getting home, so I had to walk several miles from her Maryland house to the D.C. city limits, where I could catch a bus home. Imagine how concerned I was, a young Black man walking alone on the highway at night, near many white neighborhoods. I consider myself fortunate that nothing bad happened. Needless to say, I never saw that girl again.

Once I completed my master's degree requirements in February 1961, my assistantship came to an end. Prior to that I had begun interviewing for a job with various government agencies and private companies. I realized that accepting a full-time position would torpedo my desire for a Ph.D. degree in chemistry. I was able to land a job as a research chemist at the National Institutes of Health in 1961, working under the supervision of Dr. P. S. Mueller of the Mental Health Division, while continuing my graduate coursework toward a Ph.D. That job paid enough for me to buy my first automobile, a 1956 Ford.

Before purchasing the Ford, I depended on one of my first cousins, Lawrence Harley, to provide me with transportation between Washington, D.C., and Florence. Lawrence lived in New York City and would drive down to Washington to give two or three guys a ride to Florence in his soft-top, convertible Ford. We paid him a bit, which helped defray the costs for the trips. We also shared the cost of gasoline.

As we traveled, I marveled at how his car's cloth top would push out like a balloon filled with air, and I often wondered if it would tear. There was a lack of tightness in that Ford model's roof design. We talked, laughed, ate, and slept in the car, and some of the guys—the ones Lawrence trusted—would help make the drive straight through, though we occasionally stopped to stretch our legs. Our trips usually occurred during holidays. On one particular trip, Lawrence's car heater did not work, and we had difficulty keeping warm in the midst of winter. By the time we reached Florence, I felt like a frozen piece of meat. Despite such inconveniences, none of us ever turned down the opportunity to go home.

In a stroke of great luck, an inorganic chemistry professor was looking for a research associate to carry out work required on a National Science Foundation grant, and he offered me the position after reviewing my records. This was the perfect opportunity for me, because the research would satisfy the non-coursework requirements for the terminal degree and make it possible for me to return to school full-time. This new position was going well until I lost my mother and her strong support on October 16, 1961. Her kidneys failed when she was only forty-seven years old.

In those days, older people did not see a doctor or visit a hospital until it was absolutely necessary, and then it was often too late. I was shocked by my mother's death, as I had just spent several days with her in the hospital and she had appeared to be recovering quite well. By the time I returned to Washington, however, she had passed away. Continuing in school was quite difficult for me after that, but I knew I had to succeed. Following a month of depression, I returned to the mindset required of a graduate research associate. Mom's death was also a big blow to Dad. He never married again.

PRESSING FORWARD

* * *

In late August 1963, I completed my required work for the Ph.D. degree in physical chemistry with a minor in physics, thanks to the tutelage of Dr. Kelso B. Morris. Additional good fortune came when I received an unexpected phone call from Dr. Vandon White at Southern University in Baton Rouge, about three months before completing my doctorate.

When I heard that Dr. White had called, my first reaction was to ask, "Where is Southern University?" Upon learning that it was in Louisiana, I was amazed that I had never heard of the school. Morehouse played football against several southern schools, including Dillard, Tuskegee, and Fisk. A classmate of mine from New Orleans had insisted I visit the city to partake of what he described as the best food in the world and to meet the prettiest women in the world. But not once had he mentioned Southern.

Therefore, I paid little attention to the message about a call from Dr. White. A week or so later he called again, and this time we spoke on the phone. He offered me a job as an assistant professor in Southern's chemistry department. I told him I would seriously think about it and would let him know my decision.

There were several reasons why I was uncertain about Dr. White's offer. I had an offer of a chemistry job at Morgan State University in Maryland, as well as an offer from a research laboratory in Virginia. I was seeking employment with several government agencies and had offers from several of them, including Walter Reed Army Medical Center, the Naval Research Laboratory, the Naval Ordnance Laboratory, and the National Bureau of Standards. I was also awaiting two or three responses from private companies.

I had no desire to be a teacher, and I had heard nothing but disturbing news about the state of Louisiana, especially as it related to segregation and the treatment of Blacks. (I believe that the successful imposition of "Black" over "Negro" as a designation did not occur until about 1968.) But my classmate, the New Orleanian, told me it would be a great experience. He described the fabulous food I would eat and the fine women I would meet. Additionally, Dr. Morris had spent several summers teaching at Southern. He assured me that as a faculty member at Southern, the white community would treat me with greater respect than usual. He emphasized that Southern University, a land-grant college since 1890, was a quality, historically Black public institution.

With that assurance from Dr. Morris and a desire to eat good food and to meet the prettiest women in the world, I informed Dr. White that I would accept the job at Southern. I did not tell him that I intended to stay for one year only. The Virginia research laboratory had agreed to delay my acceptance date, so my plan was to teach for a year at Southern and then head to Virginia for the laboratory job.

CHAPTER 4

Home Sweet Home, or Acclimation to Baton Rouge

So off to Louisiana I went in a brand-new 1963 Ford Galaxie, which I could now afford thanks to my new job at Southern and the prospect of working at the research laboratory in Virginia. I'd met all the requirements for my doctorate degree in August, and "all the rights and privileges appertaining thereto" were mine. I officially received my degree at Howard's 1964 spring commencement but did not attend the ceremony because of my job at Southern.

I left Washington with fond memories of one of the most significant events in history: the March on Washington for Jobs and Freedom and Martin Luther King's "I Have a Dream" speech, which occurred on August 28, 1963. I was then, and still am, proud to have been present at that event and remember so vividly the great oratory, the overwhelming camaraderie, and the goodwill shown to one another by the thousands of participants, but it took a toll on my body. I had never been so tired in my life, even when I was working in the farm fields. That day is etched in my mind.

I headed to Florence to spend time with my father before I made the long drive to Baton Rouge. Those were an enjoyable two weeks or so, and I was able to see a few friends and relatives, many of whom I had not seen since leaving South Carolina in 1955. When my visit was over, I repacked and headed down to Louisiana. It was the second week of the fall 1963 semester.

HOME SWEET HOME, OR ACCLIMATION TO BATON ROUGE

Finding a good place to stay overnight in 1963 was not easy. I spent the night in an all-Black motel in Montgomery, Alabama, and struck out for Baton Rouge the following morning. At the time, the Southern University at Baton Rouge (SUBR) was actually located in Scotlandville, a rural community along the Mississippi River about seven miles north of Baton Rouge. (Rural institutions tended to affiliate themselves with the nearest city.) Today the area is a part of the city of Baton Rouge.

I arrived at Southern at about 2 p.m., entered the chemistry building (Lee Hall), and proceeded to the department office on the second floor, where I introduced myself to the secretary, Mrs. Essie Jones. She looked at me and remarked, "I was expecting someone older, but it's good to meet you." After some chit-chat, she took me downstairs to meet the chair of the physics department. I had agreed to teach a course in physics since my academic background was in physical chemistry and physics.

The chair, Mr. Wiley W. Parker, M.S., was in class, and we went straight into the classroom to meet him. Mrs. Jones introduced me. Assistant Professor Parker immediately handed me the textbook and chalk and left the room. He didn't even tell me what he had covered before my arrival or what outline I was to follow. I had to rely on the students to steer me to the point the class had reached in the textbook. I considered his action to be totally inappropriate, but I never said a word to him about his abandoning me in that fashion. I made up my mind then and there, however, that I would never teach another class for him. And I didn't.

I met the chair of the chemistry department, Dr. Vandon White, with whom I'd first spoken on the phone, and he took me over to meet the Dean of Instruction, Dr. E. C. Harrison. Dean Harrison had to approve faculty members before they were hired. Following quite a bit of interrogation—and after Southern had verified my Ph.D.—he gave Dr. White permission to hire me as an assistant professor in the chemistry department.

I quickly developed a friendship with fellow chemistry professor Dr. Wilbur B. Clarke; he became my enthusiastic bowling partner. An urgent concern of mine was where to live. Mr. Mack Johnson, a real estate businessman whose offices were just off the Southern campus, introduced me to another SUBR faculty member from the English department, Professor

Jerome Dukes, who rented an apartment in a house on Harding Boulevard. The two of us occupied that apartment for a few months, until Mr. Johnson presented us with the opportunity to rent a small house on Pintail Street, which we took. Both of these residences were within walking distance of Southern's campus. Neither of us liked the walk, however, so my car came in very handy.

Baton Rouge is not known as an entertainment mecca, and in the 1960s and 1970s options for having fun were limited. Not only were social venues meager, but the better ones were also designated for whites. Forced to have their social activities at places within the Black community, non-whites chose places such as the Temple Theater/Roof, the Masonic Hall in Scotlandville, Lincoln Theater, Moreco's Lounge, and Triangle Lounge. Black entertainers who came to Baton Rouge stayed with Black residents or at the Black-owned Lincoln Hotel.

My position as a faculty member at Southern put me into contact with the community's elite Black residents. Dances, sorority and fraternity functions, formal affairs, and large meetings took place at the Temple Roof or Masonic Hall. I remember visiting these venues often. During one of my nights out at the Temple Roof, I was dancing the "swing-out" with a young lady and missed her hand as she twirled around. She landed on the floor. Both of us were a bit embarrassed, but I helped her up and we continued dancing.

These venues remained the focal point of Black entertainment until the construction of the Great Hall at the Bellemont Motor Lodge in 1984. The original Bellemont was an elegant structure built around 1953 along Airline Highway, the main north–south thoroughfare through Baton Rouge at the time. The Great Hall became the largest and most grand ballroom and meeting room in Baton Rouge, and it remained the entertainment center of choice until a new hotel arose near downtown Baton Rouge. In its heyday, the Bellemont was *the* place—it was where everyone wanted to go. Access to these newer facilities by the Black community came after 1964 and passage of the Civil Rights Act. Our events did not change, but their location and scale did.

HOME SWEET HOME, OR ACCLIMATION TO BATON ROUGE

When we wanted to socialize outside formal venues, we could go to Moreco's Lounge, the Triangle Lounge, and several other places. Moreco's was unique because it served as a meeting/banquet hall in addition to being a lounge. Moses McDonald was the proprietor and master chef; he prepared food only for special occasions. The College of Science at Southern regularly held its banquets at Moreco's. Some of the tastiest lobster thermidor in the world came from Moses's kitchen. He also served up porterhouse, ribeye, and T-bone steaks, as well as shrimp cocktail, bar-b-que chicken, and stuffed pork chops. Moreco's was located on Harding Boulevard, just outside Southern's campus. Amenities at venues built later were more elaborate, but they were no match for the food at Moreco's.

I never enjoyed consuming alcohol, and so I rarely frequented lounges. Many of my visits to lounges occurred during my political career, since some voters congregated at those places. The other mass gathering of potential voters was at church, and I spent a lot of time visiting houses of worship. When I wanted to experience big-time entertainment, I made a trip to New Orleans, roughly eighty miles southeast of Baton Rouge.

My first taste of a Louisiana hurricane came in 1964, when Hurricane Hilda caused severe coastal erosion, local flooding, and thirty deaths. I was uncomfortable riding out the storm in my Pintail residence, so I shared the experience with Wilbur and Neola Clarke in their house on campus. It was very kind and unexpected of them to invite me. Their home was almost directly across from the science building.

In the wake of Hurricane Hilda, the campus lost electrical power for several days. We could not cook food because the Clarkes' house had all-electric appliances. That experience convinced me that if I ever built a home, it would have natural gas appliances.

One night, a few months after I'd arrived in Baton Rouge, my roommate Jerome and I were driving home from an outing downtown. I passed a police car with two white officers in it somewhere around Scenic Highway and Choctaw Drive. I was not speeding. But the police immediately began trailing us. They followed us all the way to our house on Pintail Street and then parked down the street for several minutes after we entered the house.

Despite my sense of the racial atmosphere in Baton Rouge, I was taken aback by this surveillance. We surmised that, based on the Washington, D.C., license plate on my car, the cops pegged us as protestors from up north. Even though we believed in and supported the sit-in movement throughout the South, participating in those events was not our intent as newly arrived faculty members. I did not know about the 1960s downtown Baton Rouge lunch counter sit-ins by sixteen students from Southern. I had never even heard of Southern University before Dr. White's telephone call in the mid-summer of 1963.

Though not actively involved in the civil rights struggle, I followed its activities, and I was very aware of the various civil rights groups. I knew about the National Association for the Advancement of Colored People (NAACP), the National Urban League, the Southern Christian Leadership Conference (SCLC), the Congress of Racial Equality (CORE), and the Student Nonviolent Coordinating Committee (SNCC). Each of these groups seemed to have a somewhat different approach to the struggle, but in the end, their goals were the same: to bring about change in the way America treated minorities and the poor. I decided to adopt the NAACP as my chosen civil rights group.

Remembering Dr. Kelso B. Morris's assurance that Southern University was a quality institution of higher learning, I was proud to be a part of the chemistry department, which during the 1970s consisted of close to 22 faculty members, 16 of whom held Ph.D. degrees and 6 to 10 of whom were under the age of thirty. No other Louisiana school could boast such strength in its chemistry faculty, not even the state's flagship, Louisiana State University (LSU).

Members of Southern's chemistry faculty at that time, in alphabetical order, were Dr. Talmadge Bursh, Dr. Wilbur B. Clarke, Dr. Earl Doomes, Dr. Richard Echols, Mr. Wilton Flemming, Dr. Jack Jefferson, Dr. Julia Martin, Dr. Sidney McNairy, Dr. Robert Miller, Dr. William Moore, Dr. Ivory Nelson, Ms. Janet Pounds, Mr. Thornton Rhodes, myself, Dr. William Robinson, Dr. Spaulding Ruffin, Dr. Arnold Smalley, Dr. Mildred Smalley,

Dr. Victor Tiensu, Ms. Celestine Tillman, Mr. Charles Trotman, and Dr. Vandon White.

It was Dr. Vandon White's vision and energy that built such a powerful scientific faculty experience. This experience I call an experiment, because no school in the southern United States could match such minority faculty prowess.

Being a young and enthusiastic assistant professor of chemistry and desiring that my students not only learn the classroom material but also appreciate the contributions of chemistry to their daily lives, I began seeking one or more individuals among the department faculty who would be interested in producing a chemistry textbook designed specifically for students taking their first college course in chemistry. Such a text would be dedicated to applying chemical principles to everyday products and occurrences with which people would most likely be familiar.

Dr. Julia Martin agreed to join me in producing a book titled *Chemical Principles and Their Applications.* Students in our classes tested the text, with positive responses. I then sent the manuscript to several publishing companies, as there was no textbook of its type in print for use by classroom students. Unfortunately, I was unaware that the world of textbook publishing could be cutthroat and sometimes even deceitful, so I did not apply for a copyright for our manuscript before submitting it. To my surprise and chagrin, the major chemistry book publishers refused to accept our manuscript for publication. Some went so far as to say it was not worth publishing. Yet the following year, a book very similar to our manuscript was published by other authors. Until the day I die, I will believe they stole our concept and profited from it.

Faced with the publishers' rejections and the theft of our concept, I proceeded to seek other ways of publishing this gem of a book. In 1969, Southern University provided some bound copies, which I used in my classes. Then, in 1970, while I was doing a summer faculty internship at Eli Lilly in Indianapolis, Indiana, the company agreed to publish the book. I used it in my classes at Southern until questions arose about the ethics of the process of textbook selection. Use of our text stopped. I wonder what would have happened had the major textbook publishers not rejected the book and the concept not been stolen. With a bad taste in my mouth, I turned to other activities.

My experience at Southern University should have concluded at the end of the 1964 summer term, when I was supposed to take up a job at a Virginia research laboratory. By then, however, I no longer wanted to leave Southern. On October 9, 1964, slightly less than a year after coming to Baton Rouge, my ties to the city changed drastically: I married my wife, Ruth, who was born and raised in the capital city. I had had no intentions of getting married at the time. But I put up no resistance when Ruth said to me one night, "You mean you are going to court me for another year?" I had said something about the following year, but didn't remember it. We set the date of our wedding that night.

I likely would not have found myself in such a position had I not gone to the dentist sometime in late 1963. For Ruth Ann Washington was the dental assistant to Dr. Valerian Smith, the dentist to whom my colleagues at Southern had referred me. When I walked into the dentist's office and saw Ruth sitting at her desk, my first reaction was, "Gosh, what an attractive young lady!"

Unfortunately, though fortunately for me, visits to Dr. Smith often meant long wait times because he accepted both scheduled and unscheduled patients. So, as I waited to see the dentist, I had the opportunity to observe Ms. Washington as she responded to people in the waiting room and on the phone, as well as to Dr. Smith's need for her assistance in the exam rooms. I liked the way she carried herself.

Being somewhat shy, I didn't quite know how to approach Ruth and feared she would reject me. It took me several visits to the dentist before making a tentative move, and she was receptive to me. Before long, we were dating steadily; and suddenly we were planning our wedding. Marriage, a new house, and then a son on the way meant goodbye to the potential job prospects I had developed before leaving the Washington, D.C., area, but I had no regrets. And it did not mean that my soul was bound to Baton Rouge. I continued to seek out possible job opportunities, declining an offer from

Amoco Chemicals Corporation of Whiting, Indiana, in 1966 and from Monsanto Research Corporation of Miamisburg, Ohio, in 1968.

When Ruth and I decided to get married, we didn't tell anyone about our plans. We saw no reason to spend a lot of money on a big wedding, so we arranged to have the ceremony performed at Ruth's church, the Immaculate Conception Catholic Church in Scotlandville. We had a private ceremony, performed by Father Aubry Osborn and witnessed by three church members, which was what we wanted. Getting married near the beginning of the fall semester at Southern meant an extended honeymoon was out of the question. Instead, we took a three-day weekend trip to New Orleans, during which we were introduced to the fun part of the city. Once ensconced in the honeymoon suite at the hotel, we telephoned Ruth's mother and gave her the news. At first she was stunned and somewhat angry because we didn't let the family know ahead of the wedding so they could take part. But she and the rest of the family quickly expressed their delight in our marriage. When we called my dad to give him the news, he was just as happy for us.

I was back in the classroom at Southern the following Monday morning, and Ruth returned to her job at Dr. Smith's dental office. Such was the beginning of a beautiful marriage of fifty-four years, out of which came two sons, Press Jr. and Robin Sean. I am blessed to enjoy the love and respect of both sons' families, including five grandchildren. Press Jr. has two daughters and a son, and Robin has two sons.

I always took responsibility for handling the family finances. Ruth loved to shop at the better stores, such as Bloomingdale's, Nordstrom, Macy's, Neiman Marcus, and Dillard's. Her purchases sometimes wracked my nerves and our pocketbook, because she would often shop without telling me. I only became aware of her spending when the bill arrived. Somehow I managed to keep up with the expenses. And, I must admit, the stunning outfits she created from those shopping sprees lessened my displeasure. People would often say what a handsome couple we were, and I would stick my chest out—just a little bit.

All in all, I would characterize our marriage as wholesome, loving, and supportive. Sadly, Ruth passed away on October 29, 2018. Press Jr., Robin, and I have much to thank her for. She bore the load of making a solid family, which allowed me to pursue a career in education as well as my political and community goals. Like my dad, I have not remarried.

I remained at the Pintail address with Jerome until Ruth and I were married. She and I chose to build our home in the new Park Vista subdivision because of my quirk about not being bourgeoisie. Many employees of Southern University, including its president and other high-level administrators, resided in Southern Heights, the subdivision billed as "the place to live." Considering myself a man of the people, I wanted no part of a lifestyle different from the one I had growing up. Park Vista was only in its first filing. It was less than five minutes from campus, with cheaper lots and the pick of almost an entire street for the location of our home. Nor did it have the snooty reputation of Southern Heights. To me, Park Vista seemed the perfect place to live. Ruth and I moved into our newly built home in May 1965.

I spent a lot of time designing the interior and exterior of our new house, selecting building materials and, with Ruth, furnishing the place. I admit that I had far more say-so about the interior and exterior design than I did about the furnishings, and I was okay with that. Our Park Vista home had a gas stove and bathroom heaters, and a gas water heater. Thus, we could cook and bathe in comfort during the summer and winter whenever we lost electrical power. Yet those conveniences were not sufficient to prevent serious discomfort when the power was out, even when the appliances operated on gas. For example, some devices were gas-operated but had electric starters, and the heating and A/C did not work. The installation of a whole-house generator finally solved that issue.

The first filing of Park Vista filled up quickly. Before we knew it, the second filing was underway. The subdivision's homeowners' association, the Park Vista Improvement Association (PVIA), came into being in 1965. McHenry Jackson was its president. As members of the association, we were proud young working families with more than decent homes, attuned to maximizing and maintaining the value of our properties. Owing land/

property was very important because our forefathers had taught us that land ownership was a road to wealth.

The PVIA concerned itself with restrictions such as residential lot designations; building types, materials, and sizes; use of fences; distance between houses; set-back lines, servitudes, and requirements that each house have a carport or garage. Such housing restrictions were so important to us that we even formally mandated the type of tree that could be planted between the sidewalk and the street. Each street chose its tree type.

My Mayhaw Drive neighbors considered choosing the mayhaw tree, but rejected the idea because the tree had berries. We decided instead on the crepe myrtle, which produces beautiful flowers and has a small root system that would not interfere with sidewalks. These homeowners' values were right in line with my own, so it's no surprise that I served as the PVIA president from 1973 until 1977. It was my first leadership role in a public organization.

I never thought of myself as a leader of anything, but I experienced no encounters as subdivision president I couldn't handle. Could this have been the inaugural experience that launched my civic engagement? Perhaps it was. What one becomes in life, I believe, rests heavily on the words in Ecclesiastes 3:1—"To everything there is a season, and a time to every purpose under heaven." My life's motto is, "Never say never." No one knows when their season will arrive nor what their purpose might be.

I still live on Mayhaw Drive and am still a member of the homeowners' association. I have no regrets about my decision to live here, nor have I entertained any notion about moving away. At first, most of the households in Park Vista consisted of two people, a married couple. Soon, children became a part of each family, and we all engaged in teaching right from wrong, making time for play and togetherness, schooling, and all the other endeavors of growing a family. Our kids grew up seemingly overnight and went off to college or work. After all the time and effort to grow and raise a family, most of us found ourselves back where we began our journey, as man and wife, or perhaps as a single individual.

CHAPTER 5

Early Years at Southern

Three or four weeks into the fall 1972 semester, there was a student protest on the SUBR campus over inadequate services and edicts from the all-white Louisiana State Board of Education, which at that time was the governing authority for higher education in the state of Louisiana. One especially disturbing decree from that board limited the money per pupil that could be spent at predominantly Black SUBR to one-half of the amount spent per pupil at predominantly white LSU. This protest occurred during the period of the Black revolution. Students took their concerns to President G. Leon Netterville but did not get the response they wanted, even though for years Dr. Netterville had emphasized maintaining an open-door policy for the purpose of listening to and addressing student concerns. Thus, students decided to boycott classes for a month.

Sympathizing with their concerns, I—along with a few others from the university and the community—offered the students advice on tactics and content. We often met with the ad hoc "Students United" group led by the student activist Fred Prejean of Lafayette, Louisiana, and other students, including Rickey Hill, Malik Roman, and Charlene Hardnett. On November 15, 1972, we met with the student leaders and counseled them until the wee hours of the following morning.

We had absolutely no inkling of what was about to transpire. Prejean and three other leaders of the protest were arrested at about 2:00 a.m. on November 16 after they refused to end the boycott. By 10:30 a.m., about one thousand students were up in arms, holding a sit-in in front of the administration building in response to the arrests. Some reports claimed the student body had overtaken the president's office, shouting demands. Returning to campus after going home for lunch, I heard a radio report about the sit-in. I assumed it was occurring at Southern University at New Orleans, where demonstrations were happening daily. There couldn't be a sit-in at SUBR, I thought to myself, because that was not part of the strategy we had determined together the previous night.

Unfortunately, the report was correct. The sit-in was indeed at SUBR. If I had known of the students' actions, I would have been there with them, trying to steer them in the right direction. I often wonder what my fate might have been had I known about the sit-in. Would I have lost my life that day, like Denver Allen Smith of New Roads, Louisiana, and Leonard Douglas Brown of Gilbert, Louisiana?

To this day, the law enforcement shooter—one of the dozens to two hundred police arriving on the scene—has never been publicly identified, and the federal and state cases about the fatal shootings remain unsolved. Law enforcement personnel were on campus on the orders of Governor Edwin Edwards, at the request of the G. Leon Netterville administration, and under the direction of East Baton Rouge Parish Sheriff Al Amiss. That was a black day in the annals of the university, the parish, and the state of Louisiana, and it ended my involvement with Students United. On June 26, 1976, the Southern Board of Supervisors named the Baton Rouge campus's student union in honor of Denver Smith and Leonard Brown. It took fifty years to the day for the state of Louisiana to formally apologize for the shooting, which Governor John Bel Edwards did on November 16, 2022.

The university reopened on January 3, 1973, after closing for six weeks due to the deaths of Smith and Brown. This tragedy disrupted the students' and the university's schedules, and it took great effort by students, faculty, parents, alumni, friends, and concerned citizens to salvage the school year.

In 1996, Fred Prejean, then forty-nine years old, fought for civil rights in a far different forum—as a financial administrator in state government. He was appointed undersecretary for the Department of Wildlife and Fisheries by Governor Edwin Edwards and reappointed by Governor Mike Foster. In his student days, Prejean spoke in terms of demands and grievances. In his professional career, he measured civil rights gains in terms of minority businesses started or the number of Black employees hired. He suggested that young Black college graduates seeking policymaking roles as elected officials or as business owners and employers might be even more effective than outright protests.

At the start of my teaching career, I was amazed to teach chemistry classes of 150 or more students in a large lecture hall. But it soon became routine, and I believe I handled it well. I spent twenty-eight years—from 1963 to 1991—training students in the field of chemistry and performing chemical research.

There were limited research opportunities at Southern in the early days. The university considered itself primarily a teaching institution. Time for research was scarce due to the large class loads each teacher had to carry. Beyond that, money and space for research were nonexistent. If a space became available, one had to obtain the necessary funding by getting grants from outside agencies. Fortunately, I successfully obtained several grants during my initial years at Southern. During my later tenure, I concentrated on work assignments in various scientific areas and thus had multiple employers during summer breaks between semesters.

I was fortunate to work at such highly prestigious organizations as the General Electric Company, the Monsanto Research Corporation, the Los Alamos Scientific Laboratory, Eli Lilly, and Dow Chemical. My work assignments at General Electric during the summers of 1966 to 1968 were especially gratifying because they gave me a firsthand view of the United States space program. The Saturn V rockets, designed to lift a human-crewed spacecraft into orbit, were tested at the NASA Test Facility in Bay St. Louis, Mississippi.

During my early years at Southern, I was active in university-wide faculty issues, primarily faculty governance. I manifested my support for such issues as a member of faculty organizations on campus, such as the American Association of University Professors (AAUP) and the American Federation of Teachers (AFT). The AAUP was a national organization of college and university professors composed of teaching staff below the dean's position. The AFT was a national organization of teachers. Membership was open to all faculty members, and it was known as "the Union." I was also a strong advocate for the formation and operation of a Faculty Senate. The Faculty Senate became the official voice of the faculty, recognized by the administration and, after 1974, by the Board of Supervisors as well. It served as an advisory body to the administration on faculty welfare, governance, professional growth, freedom, and security. Membership was open to all full-time faculty members below the dean's level, as deans were considered to be part of the administration.

My College of Science faculty colleagues saw fit to elect me to represent them once the Senate was established in the fall of 1973, but its establishment was a contentious issue at the time. Initially, it was not supported by either the Felton Clark administration or some faculty members. However, colleagues such as William Moore (who became the Senate's first president), Dolores Spikes, Thomas J. Wilcox Jr., Leroy Davis, Joyce Baucom, Aaron Harris, Frances Marsh, Samuel Austin, A. L. Bowen, Dan Peterson, Ernest Simon, Spaulding Ruffin, Carolyn Jacobs, Robert Moran, Julia Martin, Leroy Roquemore, Frank Williams, Eula Masingale, Ada Belton, Ansel Creary, John Hope, Henry Stewart III, Raymond Floyd, Lloyd Nichols, John Brown, Frances Holmes, Geraldine Scott, Ira Graham, Albert McHenry, Roslyn Tolson, Clyde Johnson, and I, felt strongly that there was a need for a senate and that the faculty deserved one. We were determined to see the entity come into existence despite warnings by some fellow faculty members that our jobs might be in danger.

Looking back at that struggle, attitudes about it, and our ages at the time reminds me why young people are so active in various causes. They have no fear and often believe that "it can't happen to me." In this case, to take one example, we were right. Dolores Spikes later became president of the Faculty Senate as well as president of the Southern University system.

On November 15, 1973, a much-discussed process for naming a new Southern University system president occurred at the direction of the Louisiana State Board of Education. The board appointed a presidential search advisory committee to screen applicants. The Faculty Senate selected me to represent it as one of the three SUBR faculty members on the committee. The committee adopted a policy that the name of each applicant receiving ten or more votes would be forwarded to the State Board of Education. Five candidates achieved the required number: E. C. Harrison (17 votes), James J. Prestage (17 votes), Huel D. Perkins (10 votes), Jesse N. Stone (10 votes), and Herman Smith (10 votes).

The majority report of the committee contained only three names: Harrison, Prestage, and Perkins. The minority report, however, included the names of all five applicants. In February 1974, both reports reached the Board of Education. To many committee members' surprise and chagrin, on February 21, the board appointed Jesse N. Stone as the next president of Southern University and A&M College, effective July 1, 1974.

The selection of Jesse Stone as the president of the Southern University system is an excellent example of politicians privately making underhanded decisions. The advisory committee had worked tirelessly over many days to develop its list of recommendations, which included three individuals. We believed, on good advice, that our work was important. Almost immediately after the committee submitted its report, however, Dr. Stone was announced as the new president. Most committee members were flabbergasted and angry. We felt we had been duped, lied to, and disrespected. It looked as though the decision had already been made before the committee's report was submitted, perhaps even before the committee had been named.

Many factions of the university were dismayed by Dr. Stone's appointment, and I must admit I was among them, although our disappointment was eased somewhat by the fact that E. C. Harrison became vice president for research and planning and James Prestage was named vice president for academic affairs. Still, I suspected Dr. Stone harbored some hard feelings toward me because I had supported a different presidential candidate. Almost certainly, his advocates on the committee had told him who had or hadn't supported him. I sensed his animosity at a subsequent meeting of an administration and faculty group to which Dr. Stone had invited me. I was given a meeting time thirty minutes later than its actual start time.

When I raised a question at this meeting, I was summarily dismissed by Stone, who replied, "We already answered that question." He then referred to my being late and proceeded to move forward with the meeting, paying no attention to my explanation about the meeting time I received.

It seemed such a small thing for him to do. Later, I got a message that Dr. Stone had said words to the effect that I "had better get off his back," to which I responded, "If he is worried about 'little old me' being on his back, what will he do when the major trouble comes his way?" Major trouble seemed sure to come from both faculty and students. I was no longer invited to such meetings. But, as far as I know, there were no further consequences that came my way.

As a side note, one of Stone's first acts as president was to appoint advisory committee member Clarence Marie Collier as system vice president for student affairs and community services. I am not saying that was a bad choice, simply that Collier knew the end game and participated in the charade. Collier is believed to be the first woman to become a college vice president in Louisiana and the first woman to hold such a position in student personnel services in the country.

I surmised then, and still believe, that the State Board of Education felt comfortable taking the action it did because its members knew that the board's existence was at an end with the advent of the 1974 state constitution. Under newly elected Governor Edwin W. Edwards, the 1974 state constitution established new administrative boards for institutions of higher education, including a Board of Supervisors for the newly formed Southern University system. The campuses in Baton Rouge, New Orleans, and Shreveport (a two-year school), the Southern Agricultural Research and Extension Center, and the Southern Law Center were all members of the group. Today, the system still consists of the original five campuses.

Some of the frustration created by the state board's decision was evident at the first meeting of the Southern University Board of Supervisors in May 1975. Two board members, Walter Dumas and Rev. Lionel Johnson, who were rivals for election as board chairman, repeatedly clashed at the meeting, and a resolution that gave the board's support to the president of the system eventually passed 9–1 with 4 abstentions (only 14 members of the 17-member board attended the meeting). Board member Basile Miller of Lake Charles—a trusted friend of Stone—raised the first objection to the resolution by noting that the present board had no part in naming Stone as president. He did not want the board to pass what sounded like a statement of political support for Stone, who maintained that the resolution neither came from his office nor had his support. Stone did say, however, that he did not believe he could function in the university's best interests if he lacked the board's confidence.

Over the next several years President Stone faced other resistance from the board. He came under political pressure from State Representative Joseph A. Delpit and State Senator Richard Turnley, both of Baton Rouge. Most of their criticism involved the university's handling of a sports contract. In October 1984, Stone announced his desire for a three-year contract with Southern to help him fight off his political opposition. According to Stone, students had told him that some outsiders had been trying to give them money to put into their student campaigns in order to influence them on matters that came before the board. Rev. Lionel Johnson Sr., who served as the chairman of the Board of Supervisors, said, "I don't know of any legal basis for giving a contract to a university president. I would be unalterably opposed to a three-day contract, let alone a three-year contract, for a university president. I would refuse to put it on the agenda. The board would have to compel me by majority vote to put it on."

Stone intended to present his request to the full board at its November 3, 1984, meeting, but in the end said he didn't feel comfortable bringing it up. By that meeting, the Rev. Lionel Johnson—previously one of Stone's staunchest supporters—had called for his ouster. Johnson said he hoped the board would support Stone's removal for the good of Southern. If it didn't, he would seriously consider quitting his chairmanship. The controversy deepened. Ultimately, Stone announced his resignation during the week of February 17, 1985, to be effective September 1. The Board of Supervisors unanimously accepted his resignation at its March 2 meeting.

During his tenure as president of the Southern system, Stone often found himself in conflict with faculty and students alike. He was at odds with the student newspaper, *The Digest,* for example, during the 1975 spring semester. The *Digest* editors and advisers accused Stone of retaliating because they had criticized him. In an exchange between Stone, the university comptroller, and *Digest* adviser Ansel Creary, Stone pronounced Creary "personally repugnant" and refused to work with him.

In another example, Robert Ford, elected president of the Faculty Senate in 1979 for a two-year term and re-elected for another two years in 1981, alleged in a suit against Stone that he had attained the status of tenured professor at Southern but was denied promotion without just cause and in violation of his right of free speech. Moreover, the suit alleged, Ford was discharged without just cause in May 1981. As Faculty Senate president, Ford frequently voiced faculty opposition to university policies and practices; he also made recommendations and proposals on the faculty's behalf.

It is safe to say that I never gained the trust and respect in President Stone that I had hoped to place in the first system president. My characterization of him shortly after the beginning of his administration as "small" and "vindictive" seemed to make itself manifest. Recognizing the historical significance of "firsts," however, Stone deserves accolades for several achievements. He was a member of the Southern University Law School's inaugural graduating class, and he was one of the first Black lawyers in Shreveport, where he handled a number of civil rights cases. Prior to his appointment as Southern's president, he served as the first Southern law graduate to be appointed dean of the law school. Moreover, Stone was the first Black to be appointed as an associate justice of the Louisiana State Supreme Court, serving from 1972 to 1974.

In the early 1970s, a group of Southern University engineers sought to form an engineering consultant firm, and they asked me, a non-engineer, to join. When I asked why they had invited me, they said I could bring some balance to the group. I strongly suspect, however, that they included me because I voluntarily taught their students the chemistry part of the Engineer in Training (EIT) exam review. Currently referred to as the Fundamentals of Engineering (FE) exam, it represents the first of two examinations that engineers must pass to be licensed as professional engineers in the United States.

I joined the group. In August 1972, we became the first minority-owned and -operated consulting engineering firm south of Atlanta, Georgia, and east of California. Our next task was to name the firm. I proposed Minority Engineers of Louisiana, Incorporated (MEL), which the group adopted. The firm still exists and bears that name.

My initial role as a member of the firm's board of directors eventually morphed into my serving as a project manager on environmental work, as chief administrative officer for more than forty-one years, and as vice president for much of the firm's existence. I retired from MEL twice. My first retirement occurred on August 15, 1991, when the company was completely reorganized and restructured. Still, I continued to provide computer data input and report preparation services after my regular working hours and on weekends. I remained associated with the company at that level until September 2005, when I rejoined the firm as vice president and chief administrative officer. I retired from MEL for the second time in 2013.

MEL consisted of around one hundred employees at its peak, which was during the firm's design of the Alexandria, Louisiana, section of Interstate Highway 49 (I-49). The firm offered inspection, surveying, and environmental services, as well as mechanical, electrical, and civil engineering. The U.S. Army Corps of Engineers awarded a large portion of the firm's work in the inspection and surveying categories. In contrast, most work in the engineering disciplines was awarded by state and local governments. There were also occasional jobs for private companies and entities.

The biggest project MEL performed for the Corps was to provide inspection services during the debris cleanup for the area north of Airline Highway in New Orleans following the widespread flooding and destruction caused by Hurricane Katrina, which came ashore on August 29, 2005. This project required fifty inspectors, who were tasked to certify that cleanup contractors hauled away the actual amount and type of debris they claimed for reimbursement. Those work assignments were dramatic and gut-wrenching due to the extent of the devastation. Some were flat-out tragic, as when inspectors from New Orleans discovered the remains of family and community members in the debris. The Corps rated MEL's work highly, which represented their continued satisfaction with the firm's performance for more than forty years.

I fondly remember how proud the Corps' contract negotiator was when he finally computerized his office. We were able to modify proposed contract calculations utilizing Microsoft Excel and telephone conferencing easily and quickly. Before that time, the Corps conducted all analyses by hand, which usually meant in-person negotiations. Morgan M. Watson, long-time president of MEL, was my partner; he was one of the original engineering faculty from Southern. Even today, he still operates the firm and maintains his affiliation with engineering students' training at the university.

MEL's development into a viable engineering consultant firm benefited from its certification as a legitimate Minority Business Enterprise by the state of Louisiana and the local government. Even more important was the firm's certification as an 8(a) Minority-Owned Small Business, which made it possible for MEL to participate in the federal government's required 5 percent contract set-aside program for such certified businesses.

Almost immediately, however, we encountered difficulties in winning contract awards because white-owned companies, which did not qualify for the 8(a) program, formed bogus minority-owned companies with a minority individual as a figurehead in order to qualify for certification. Moreover, some federal agencies balked at setting contracts aside for minorities.

Other shenanigans also marginalized minority contractors. For example, when the New Orleans branch of the Army Corps of Engineers finally awarded a sizable surveying contract to MEL, the contract—which was historically awarded at the $1 million level—suddenly was broken up into pieces, with a $400,000 maximum. We found ourselves battling competition both from bogus businesses and federal agencies, proving that discrimination was everywhere and was seriously hindering MEL's growth and development.

My first foray into project and administrative management came about because of my involvement at MEL. There, I honed my planning, organizing, scheduling, and performing work just as I had done with my chemical research projects. I had little to no experience in managing people and finances, and MEL allowed me to learn those skills on the job. I discovered that I could manage with objectivity, honesty, and consistency.

At the same time, my partner Watson leaned toward the "big heart and grand ideas" approach to management, which resulted in unnecessary problems. During the 1980s, for example, he decided to set up an office in Shreveport without consulting me about logistics or finances. When I learned of the move and conducted a financial analysis, it became clear that MEL could not afford to open the Shreveport office without a tremendous drain on its resources. Nonetheless, Watson had created the office, hired personnel, and rented space. It took me five years and a considerable amount of money to reverse those actions.

Unfortunately, Watson's management style and grandiose ideas were common occurrences. His favorite saying was, "It's better to ask for forgiveness than to ask for permission." Analyzing the financials, as well as other aspects of commercial decisions, is not asking for permission; it's operating under sound business principles. But Watson was and remains a spellbinding salesman. He professed to work by "dazzling people and agencies with brilliance and baffling them with bullshit."

One of the strangest occurrences in the annals of MEL was a revolt by a segment of our office staff. It occurred one day when our comptroller challenged me about a relatively unimportant matter, and I suggested that he drop the subject. Instead of letting it go, he challenged me even more. The situation escalated to the point that I ordered him to leave the office. When he finally followed my directive and left, I suspended him. Ultimately, I fired him for insubordination, whereupon several administrative staffers walked out to support his position.

I immediately told those employees that if they were not back at work after a specified time, I would consider them to have abandoned their positions and they would be terminated. Realizing that I was determined in my warning, most of them returned within the time frame stipulated. The comptroller, of course, had no option to return. This disruption to MEL's operations was uncalled for, and to my relief, nothing similar ever occurred again. To this day, I am genuinely uncertain as to what caused the situation.

Being an active participant at MEL was a pleasure, and I spent many joyful hours keeping its administrative functions operating efficiently and effectively. In 2013, however, MEL's unexplained involvement in Haiti following the devastating 7.0 earthquake of 2010, which affected 3 million people and left 1.5 million homeless, forced me to resign my vice presidency and CAO positions. I had no part in MEL's work in Haiti, and my partner refused to give me an explanation about the nature of the firm's activities there. Nor did I have an understanding of the monetary, legal, or work requirements involved. So I decided to retire.

CHAPTER 6

Wings beyond the University

Almost immediately after arriving at Southern, I'd begun to ask about the university's involvement in the community—specifically, the Scotlandville community. I learned that there was little, if any, such involvement. In fact, it was suggested to me that I should not freely associate with the population outside the campus. I repeatedly suggested to various school officials that we—for I was now a part of the school—should engage with the Scotlandville populace and bring about cooperative endeavors. No one seemed interested.

So I began developing my own activities. Around 1970, I became involved with the Scotlandville Advisory Council (SAC), then chaired by Richard Turnley and composed of citizens of Scotlandville, who served as consultants to the Scotlandville Neighborhood Service Center. The center was a branch of Community Advancement, Inc. (CAI), the parish's antipoverty agency, formed in 1965 after federal economic opportunity legislation passed during the Lyndon B. Johnson administration. That legislation brought about the creation of the Community Action Programs, supposedly designed to stamp out poverty.

Under executive director Charlie W. Tapp, CAI operated service centers in Scotlandville, Eden Park, and South Baton Rouge. SAC's interests were issues confronting the Scotlandville area, such as a proposed expressway, traffic control in a residential section known as the Avenues, upgrades to Anna T. Jordan Park, and pollution of the Monte Sano Bayou. These issues and others were raised during meetings that ultimately fostered greater involvement of Scotlandville residents in decisions and developments that directly affected them and the area in which they lived.

Tapp, a white male, came to the fledgling CAI organization when it was common practice to name a white individual to head an agency and a Black individual to be the assistant. Percy Sims, a Black man, was named as the agency's assistant; he held the title of associate director. In early March 1972, Tapp resigned—initially effective April 1 and then May 31. The reasons for his resignation were unclear. He may have left because of a critical federal General Accounting Office audit of some of the agency's operations and procedures, several years of on-again, off-again picketing by Blacks that was fraught with racial implications, or honest differences of opinion between him and some of the board members.

The CAI's board of directors consisted of seventeen members appointed by the East Baton Rouge City-Parish Council; seventeen members from business, labor, and other community organizations; and eighteen members either from or representing the CAI's target communities. Led by President Matthew Pitts, the board planned to name Tapp's successor in June 1972. Three CAI administrative staff members, all of whom were Black, were interested in the executive directorship: Charlie Granger, Ed Popleon, and Lee Wesley.

Wesley became the new executive director and oversaw the agency until its liquidation in October 1977 following a bitter political struggle that pitted Joseph Delpit, Richard Turnley, Kevin Reilly, Pearl George, Jewel Newman, and several other state and local politicians against Mayor W. W. "Woody" Dumas, his administration, and Councilman Howard Marsellus.

After CAI's liquidation, several former officers formed the private group Human Resources and Development, Inc. (HRDI). HRDI administered several of CAI's former programs. Dumas and the city-parish council created a competing city-parish replacement, the Baton Rouge Association for Community Action (BRACA). As a former member of the CAI board of directors since 1971, I became HRDI's president, serving alongside former CAI board members Audrey Jackson as secretary and John Hope as treasurer.

Meanwhile, members of SAC and I remained committed to improving the living conditions of the people of Scotlandville. Working with the community, particularly with the Anna T. Jordan Recreation Council, my SAC colleagues and I soon realized that political involvement was necessary if we were to have a meaningful impact on the issues at hand. Because of its ties to federal and local governments, it was unlawful for SAC to pursue political activities. Thus, in 1968, the Scotlandville Area Advisory Council (SAAC) came into existence. SAAC was a community organization with both civic and political aspirations, and it was registered with the Louisiana Secretary of State on March 3, 1974.

SAAC played an extraordinary role in the political and civic experiences I have had in the Baton Rouge area. As chairman of the Education Committee of SAAC, I was highly involved in all of the organization's efforts to inform the citizens of the Scotlandville area, the city of Baton Rouge, and the rest of East Baton Rouge Parish. SAAC and other legitimate Black political groups were successful not only in the Baton Rouge area, but also throughout the state of Louisiana. Some individuals outside the Black communities believed Black voters were voting as political bosses told them to do.

On the contrary, Black political groups were successful because they evaluated candidates and issues. They provided long-term, year-round services, such as giving Blacks access to the system and making recommendations to voters. The winning candidates they supported did a respectable job of representing their Black constituents, providing a pathway for Blacks to influence decisions made by public officials. Winning elections for Black candidates as well as securing jobs and business opportunities for Blacks were the main priorities of these groups.

Like other members of the electorate, Black voters vote for what is in their best interest. People who paint Black political groups as "shakedown artists" are not concerned about the welfare of Black voters; they are upset because Black voters often determine who gets elected or who does not. To keep Black voters and Black elected officials outside the game of governance and decision-making, white voters often try to sow doubt and confusion. They listen to news reports about investigations of voter fraud and loudly voice suspicions that candidates are buying off Black political groups. It seems as if the white political establishment changes the rules of the game every time Blacks learn to operate successfully within the system.

Admittedly, some Black political groups were sloppy, fly-by-night, and even dishonest. But Black voters were smart enough to know which groups provided legitimate, practical campaign tools. The legitimate groups offered a candidate, particularly a white candidate, an established grass-roots organization and instant credibility in a community they could not otherwise hope to influence. Furthermore, these organizations formed a formidable parish-wide base of advocacy for both the Black community and the community at large through their organized collective actions. They utilized every resource available to them to solve the problems affecting a too-long-ignored segment of the community.

Key characteristics of parish-wide organization were collective consideration of issues and concerns and the selection of a single spokesperson to articulate the group's positions. Some attempts to organize were not successful. In 1968, for example, a parish-wide meeting was held in an attempt to form an effective community activities force. The meeting bogged down due to bickering between different age and area groups. Sadly, there were conflicts between the older attendees and the younger ones. Though not the only source of dissension, naming the group proved to be a sore point. Insults were hurled at some of the older leaders by some of the younger folks in attendance, and two young men walked out. In the end, such enmity sabotaged the effort, and the intended group never formed. Luckily, the parish-wide organization of elected officials continued to operate effectively.

I wish to pay special attention to some of the memorable events in which I participated where SAAC had measurable involvement and outcomes. These events all have a fundamental bearing on the day-to-day lives of the residents of Black communities.

The first of these events involved the desire of some parish and city officials to build an east–west runway at Baton Rouge's Ryan Airport. The airport has been located near the predominantly Black area of East Baton Rouge Parish known as Scotlandville for many years. Around 1958, Ryan officials began to discuss building a new airport runway and making other upgrades as well. A runway plan received approval in 1959 but was abandoned in 1965 and grounded by the City-Parish Council on July 6, 1966. It was reactivated on July 13 of that year after the Federal Aviation Agency (FAA) and commercial airlines warned that existing facilities at Ryan were inadequate for modern jet aircraft. On June 28, 1967, the City-Parish Council approved spending $1.6 million in excess revenue bonds to construct an 8,000-foot runway, which was then vetoed by Mayor Woody Dumas. His veto was overridden by the City Council (not the City-Parish or Parish Council, neither of which had enough votes to override the mayor's veto) on July 12, 1967.

This timeline is supported by the fact that the city-parish denied three applications from the school board for a permit to build Ryan Elementary School on the northwest corner of Elm Grove Garden Drive and Progress Road: the first application sometime between 1960 and 1965, the second in 1965, and the third on September 21, 1967. The City-Parish Council finally authorized the issuance of a permit for the construction of Ryan Elementary School in what would be the clear zone of the proposed east–west runway on June 2, 1968. The construction permit was finally issued in October 1968. The school was finally completed on July 24, 1969.

In addition to the proposed school, improvements to a major Scotlandville thoroughfare, Elm Grove Garden Drive, were held up because the project fell within the clear zone of the proposed east–west runway. Residents in the Elm Grove Garden Drive vicinity felt the street upgrades were so crucial that Black leaders threatened a lawsuit when the parish discontinued preliminary work on the project in 1967. The suit, filed in state and federal district courts on August 17, 1967, sought continuation of the road project.

Meanwhile, large numbers of Scotlandville residents objected to the runway project because it would result in the closure of Elm Grove Garden Drive, the only thoroughfare between Plank Road and Scenic Highway that ran entirely through Scotlandville. They also objected because jet planes would be flying directly over their homes and schools. There were two schools on Elm Grove Garden Drive—Harding Elementary and Scotlandville Middle—and none of the six schools in the Scotlandville community were more than one and a quarter miles from the clear zone of the runway.

Following a meeting between FAA and local officials on October 20, 1967, Acie Belton and I, representing the Black residents opposed to the runway, visited FAA headquarters in Dallas, Texas, and met with officials there to understand why federal funds to help finance the runway had been deferred, and to once again present our objections to the east–west runway project.

The Second Ward Voters League, the First Ward Voters League, state and local branches of the NAACP, and city-parish activists all strongly opposed the proposed runway. On March 14, 1968, Black leaders met with city-parish officials to warn that violence might occur if some actions were not taken. The meeting was called for by Emmitt C. Douglas, state president of the NAACP; Joseph Delpit, president of the Baton Rouge chapter; Larry Dyson, local NAACP Youth Council president; and community activist Pearl George.

This meeting was the first known confrontation between Black community members and locally elected officials to which the Biracial Committee (a city-parish committee that intervened on issues involving race) was not invited. Richard Turnley, Kenneth Joseph, other Scotlandville residents, and I were members of the Second Ward Voters League and wholeheartedly supported opposition to the east–west runway. We also supported many of the delays in the construction of the elementary school and upgrades to Elm Grove Garden Drive. The Elm Grove thoroughfare would have had to be relocated if the runway had been built.

In a bitter floor fight over the aviation issue on June 12, 1968, the City-Parish Council, in a 6–4 vote, dealt a disabling blow to the proposal for an east–west runway at Ryan Airport. Raymond P. Scott, a Black resident from South Baton Rouge, commenting on the back-and-forth votes, said,

"Yesterday I saw honorable men discuss an issue, and their attitude toward tanks was more kind than toward people." His remark referred to the airport commission's opposition to a northwest–southeast runway because an oil tank farm would be in the clear zone.

At the City-Parish Council's June 26, 1968, meeting, two long-time proponents of the east–west runway asked the council to abandon all moves to build the strip and admitted that "it's over and done with. It's a foregone conclusion." The council voted unanimously that day to abandon the project.

Proponents of the new runway had declared that the east–west project was the only possible solution to the aviation dilemma in the parish. There was, they said, no alternative. Oddly enough, Baton Rouge Metropolitan Airport (formerly Ryan) is now an updated regional facility that provides adequate service to the metropolitan area and easily accommodates jet aircraft.

Another event with which I was involved as a member of SAAC was the Acme Brick strike. On February 10, 1969, forty-seven Black employees of Acme Brick Company, now known as Justin Industries, Inc., went on strike at the Scenic Highway plant north of Scotlandville. The strike followed an impasse in contract negotiations between the firm and the International Union of District 50, United Mine Workers of America.

Negotiations had been ongoing since the preceding summer, but union officials said there was little chance of an early settlement. They blamed the management's unwillingness to negotiate in good faith. That appeared to be the case because Acme hired a new crew to replace the men who went on strike. Of the thirty replacements, twenty-six were white men from outside the area.

Jody Bibbins, representing the Student Union at Southern University, said the Acme workers received "slave wages." He noted that although 85 percent of the strikers had worked at Acme for twelve or more years, including some who had up to twenty-five years of service, they were making only $1.60 an hour and had received an offer of about $1.70 based upon a not very well defined or well understood merit system. Bibbins also said that men working the assembly line were paid only 18 cents per 1,000 bricks.

Evans Sanders, a spokesman for Acme, said the strikers had asked for a 40-cent-per-hour raise and better working conditions. A Help Wanted advertisement in the *Baton Rouge State-Times* published February 24 stated that Acme Brick Company was currently interviewing both experienced and inexperienced production workers, laborers, machine operators, and equipment operators. Maintenance men were also needed. The advertisement further specified that the company offered good wages ($1.72–$2.82 an hour), free employee insurance, paid vacations, paid holidays, and other fringe benefits. Steady employment with a reliable, well-established company was promised, and plenty of work was available.

Along with several other organizations, including the First Ward Voters League and the Southern Christian Leadership Conference, SAAC joined the striking workers with the intention of bringing about a settlement. We assisted in providing food and other necessities for the strikers and their families. Unfortunately, eighteen LSU and Southern students (four of whom were women) were arrested on March 6 when they tried to block access to the Acme plant in support of the strikers. Nine of them were released on $1,000 bond apiece, and nine others spent the night in jail before being released. The students were critical of the firm and what they claimed was indifference from then-Governor John McKeithen and other state and labor officials.

On Friday, April 18, local NAACP president Dr. D'Orsay Bryant called for a boycott of the company's products in order to force a settlement of the dispute. Dr. Bryant accused the company of paying its Black employees "slave wages" while sending large profits back to its home office in Texas. He helped the strikers instigate a suit with the Equal Employment Opportunities Commission (EEOC).

A union official, John Courtney, said that "because of the NAACP and our letters, there have been loads and loads of bricks turned back, and it has really hurt the company." He maintained that the only thing that kept the business operating was shipping a large number of bricks outside the area, "beyond the influence of the boycott."

The three-month strike at Acme Brick Company of Baton Rouge ended Wednesday, May 21, 1969, when an agreement was reached between company officials and the negotiating committee of the United Mine Workers of America District 50 local. Striking employees were to return to work as quickly as job assignments materialized. It was not clear how long it would take for the plant to be at full force, presumably because many of its former employees left the Baton Rouge area to work elsewhere after the strike began.

On August 4, 1975, a discrimination suit was filed against Acme Brick by Lionel McCastle, who sought $50,000, saying he had worked for Acme for fourteen years as a laborer-setter. The suit charged that prior to the strike that began on February 10, 1969, the workforce was entirely Black. Immediately after the strike, according to the suit, Acme discharged its Black employees and replaced them with white employees who were brought on at a higher rate of pay. McCastle further claimed that at the time of his discharge, Acme practiced systematic discrimination against Blacks by refusing to promote them or employ them as supervisors or foremen.

On September 25, 1975, Hezekiah Carter likewise filed a $75,000 civil rights suit in U.S. District Court against Acme, contending that white employees were systematically hired to replace Blacks following the 1969 strike.

Another important event during my SAAC involvement was the planning and construction of the 8.6 miles of I-110 roadway that extended from I-10 in downtown Baton Rouge to Scenic Highway, US 61 north of Scotlandville. The undertaking began in 1954 and finally reached completion in 1984.

SAAC was very active during this project's planning stage, working with residents of Scotlandville and surrounding neighborhoods. It saw its role as presenting local residents' desires to officials and keeping the community informed about various aspects of the construction process, such as property sales and acquisitions, as well as relocation benefits and assistance. The group's track record was not flawless. In March 1973, several officials held a meeting for the stated purpose of discussing the problems of residents who would be impacted by the project. That meeting did not bring those problems into the open. Nor did it call for area residents to attend, submit complaints, or ask questions. Those in charge banned news reporters from the meeting. Instead, the officials went into executive session and only provided a news release to the public afterward.

But SAAC ultimately succeeded in working with local communities. The group was determined to see that the highway through the area would not be an ugly steel-and-concrete monster. Furthermore, SAAC wanted a guarantee that the community would have ready access to the road. Back when I-10 was built through Baton Rouge, the Black neighborhood of Valley Park was impacted for the worse: the only through streets past I-10 were College Drive, Acadian Thruway, and Nairn Drive. Seven or more streets in Valley Park had their terminus adjacent to either side of the interstate highway, and such cut-offs seriously restricted movement in and through that community. North Baton Rouge neighborhoods were having none of that. We made ourselves heard whenever the opportunity presented itself.

After some back-and-forth between area residents and local, state, and federal officials, planners proposed to minimize the number of blocked-off streets by constructing a raised freeway instead of building at ground level and to adopt a new concept for the construction of the Scotlandville bypass. The design, known as a "joint use program," was among the first of its kind in the nation. It allowed for the usage of land beneath and alongside the elevated portions of the freeway for local benefits, such as parks, playgrounds, picnic areas, sandboxes, shelters, and bike paths.

This design plan alleviated one of the prime complaints about America's vast interstate highway system: it took up too much land that could have been put to better purposes. The strongest criticism of the plan concerned the empty spaces beneath the elevated portions of the interstate. Perhaps because of the criticism, perhaps because of better reasoning, and perhaps because of SAAC's insistence that the freeway add value to our communities, special efforts were made to utilize much of that dead space to benefit nearby residents.

The decision to allow the use of such space did not come easily; some federal and local officials resisted at first. Financing issues arose. Issues also arose when the federal, state, and city governments tried to work together. The East Baton Rouge Recreation and Park Commission (known as BREC) entered into an agreement with the state Department of Highways to maintain the recreational areas. The inclusion of recreational and beautification facilities as a part of the freeway construction process demonstrated to residents that their lives and surroundings were important, thus easing their acceptance of I-110.

My service with the Legal Aid Society (LAS) of Baton Rouge also occurred during my time with SAAC. I served as a board member of LAS from about 1971 to 1975 and as board chairman from 1975 to 1977. LAS consisted of legal aid or pro bono attorneys, who provided legal assistance for little or no cost to low-income clients facing legal problems. Black clients constituted a very sizable fraction of the people served. Yet there were no Black members of the LAS board of directors until 1966, when Audrey Kennedy, Louis Jetson, and Acie Belton were appointed to the board by the Baton Rouge Bar Association.

Before their appointment, the LAS was a legal aid group in which a majority of the members belonged to the local bar. As a result, the bar association controlled the actions of LAS with minimal input from its client constituency, primarily the poor and/or minority. Only the threat of a competing federal government agency led to the Black appointments.

By the time I became a board member, many complaints faced the agency. Some criticism revolved around the large number of attorneys on the 40-member board of directors, in contrast to the small number of staffers. Appointments such as mine attempted to correct the board membership so that LAS's client constituency had a significant voice in the society's activities. But, as of December 1977, the board of directors' membership stood at 27 attorneys and only 13 representatives of the client community. The board was not in compliance with federal regulations.

A regional report on LAS by the Legal Services Corporation, the federal agency that funded and oversaw the nation's Legal Aid Societies, called the Baton Rouge board "unmanageable and inefficient." What's more, a regional specialist informed the society in 1976 that since fourteen members had been appointed to the board by the Baton Rouge Bar Association, the local bar had a "domineering" influence on the board.

Another criticism was that Legal Aid attorneys had too many cases. The society did not try to educate the public about its services or indeed its very existence, since it did not want new business. The board held only four meetings a year and a quorum was rarely attained, yet the board exerted extraordinary control over the direction of the program. Its decision making was cumbersome, as its membership was comprised of many special interest groups. The regional report also contained allegations that funds were not appropriately handled in 1976, and that there was a lack of communication between the director and staff, as well as low morale, which resulted in heavy staff turnover.

As the chairman of the board of directors, I intended to correct the problems listed in the regional report, as well as other problems that we identified ourselves. By November 1977, I was convinced that we could work out an agreement with the Baton Rouge Bar Association to limit its number of representatives on the board. Further, I hoped the board would become much more active than it had been in the previous two years, and that it would work harder to bring the agency more in line with what federal Legal Services required.

On February 27, 1978, an active board of directors voted and approved a proposal to the general membership that included several changes to the society. First, the board voted to change the organization's name from the Legal Aid Society of Baton Rouge to the Capital Area Legal Services Corporation—an appropriate step, since the society's task was to serve the 55,000 persons living at or below poverty levels in East and West Baton Rouge Parishes.

The proposal also reduced the board from 40 to 30 members: 18 attorneys and 12 laypersons. The attorneys were selected by the Baton Rouge Bar Association, the Louis A. Martinet Legal Society, the 18th Judicial District Bar Association, the Southern University and LSU law school deans, and the board of directors of Legal Aid.

The laypersons were chosen by the Baton Rouge Association for Community Action, Lemoyne Community Action in West Baton Rouge Parish, the East Baton Rouge Council on Aging, and the Legal Aid Society Board. As of February 27, 1978, current members of the board were to serve until July 1 of that year, when the proposed new board was in place and certified. New board members would then serve until January 1, 1980, or until the election of their successors.

My tenure as the board president ended in February 1978. Martin Bellar became the new board president, charged with putting our proposal into action and, above all, properly providing legal services to the disadvantaged populations of the Baton Rouge area, while ensuring that its clients had representation at every level of the agency, especially in its board of directors.

Another event I wish to describe relates directly to the primary reason that SAAC was established: to influence elected and appointed officials when they were making decisions that impacted the lives of people and communities. We contended that Blacks needed to be a part of the system to have an influential voice in what happens in our lives and communities. Such involvement in the system is as important today as it was then.

On August 2, 1971, Richard Turnley announced his candidacy for one of the eight East Baton Rouge Parish seats in the Louisiana House of Representatives. Among his accomplishments, he listed his presidency of SAAC and of the Anna T. Jordan Recreation Council. At the time, I was away for the summer, working at Los Alamos Scientific Laboratory in Los Alamos, New Mexico. Upon my return to Baton Rouge, I was immediately energized by Turnley's candidacy and asked what I could do to assist. At the time, Joseph Delpit of Ward 1, elected in the 1968 general election, was the only Black elected official in the parish. Black citizens were ready and eager to campaign for a cause we felt was long overdue. That cause was to elect additional Black officials. Along with others, I was pleased with our efforts, which resulted in the election that year of Representatives Johnnie A. Jones in District 67 and Turnley in the newly created District 63.

In keeping with that philosophy, SAAC supported Al Amiss for sheriff of East Baton Rouge Parish in the election of July 1972. The council encouraged Amiss to hire Black deputies, set up a substation in Scotlandville, and appoint the first Black sheriff's captain and substation commander.

When Sheriff Amiss took office, there were only a few Black deputies. When he died in office, there were a proportionate number of Black deputies compared to the parish's Black population. The temporary location of the Scotlandville substation on Scotland Avenue opened on March 31, 1973. Dalton Honore was the first Black sheriff's deputy promoted to captain. He was the first Black substation commander in the parish.

Honore had been a deputy from 1965 to 1968 and returned to the sheriff's office when Amiss was elected in 1972. Honore then served as the Scotlandville substation commander until 1978, when he was replaced by another Black officer, Lieutenant Thomas Fluker. Fluker was later promoted to captain along with two white lieutenants. It was essential that, once elected, candidates supported by our organization kept their campaign commitments to operate in the best interests of Black citizens. We monitored such activities to make sure those commitments were honored.

SAAC's efforts to get Black officials elected and appointed to prominent positions of influence did not end with the first Black sheriff captain and substation commander. When SAAC supported Edwin W. Edwards in his winning campaign for governor of Louisiana in 1984, it urged him to name Blacks to prominent positions in his administration. One such position chosen by the Edwards administration was the Department of Labor's Office of Employment Security; they tapped Dr. George Whitfield, SAAC's public relations director and speechwriter to head the office. Other state-level appointments supported by the Black political organizations were Griffin Rivers, deputy secretary, Department of Corrections; Dr. Charles Hudson, deputy secretary, Department of Transportation and Development; James W. Lee Jr., assistant secretary, Office of Minority Affairs; Clarence Cunningham, undersecretary, Office of Minority Affairs; J.W. Vaughn, assistant secretary, Office of Community Services; Mitchell Albert Jr. (SAAC), assistant secretary, Office of State Clearinghouse; and Ferguson Brew (SAAC), deputy assistant secretary, Office of Consumer Protection, Department of Urban and Community Affairs.

Most of these Black appointments were firsts for the state of Louisiana, and I want to add that this list is not an exhaustive roster of all Blacks who served in Governor Edwards's administration. Governor Edwards made an honest attempt to fulfill his campaign promises to place more women and Blacks in state government positions.

SAAC continued its push for Black-appointed positions with Baton Rouge Mayor-President Pat Screen. Shortly after taking office in January 1981, Screen named SAAC vice president and political action committee chairman Kenneth Joseph as assistant director of purchasing. This appointment marked another first for Blacks. By May 16, 1987, seven men, including Black fireman Thomas Woods, had passed the civil service exam for Baton Rouge fire chief. Woods, acting Baton Rouge fire chief as of April 1, 1987, was named the permanent fire chief on May 27 of that year. He was the first Black to hold that position.

In announcing the appointment, Mayor Screen said, "This appointment is a clear signal to the nation that we are ready to assume a leadership role in the New South. I want the message to go out to all that it is the level of an individual's professional skills and the quality of one's character, not the color of one's skin or ethnic background, that results in a person becoming a leader in the public and private sectors of our community."

As was the case with each individual supported by SAAC for an appointed position, Woods not only had high qualifications but also the temperament suitable for his position. He had started fighting fires in 1956 with the Scotlandville Fire Department and had reached the rank of captain by 1958. The Scotlandville department later merged with the city fire department, and in 1979 Woods was appointed the Baton Rouge Fire Department's chief training officer. His strong qualifications then propelled him to a District 2 Metro Council seat, representing the Scotlandville area, in 1988.

SAAC never lost sight of its goal to elect Black individuals to meaningful local and state positions. We were successful in getting elected SAAC members Richard Turnley, state representative (1972–1984) and state senator (1984–1988); Jewel J. Newman, city-parish councilman (1973–1983) and state representative (1984–1988); myself as school board member (1980–2002); and Henry Allen, justice of the peace (1976–1983). SAAC's support of both Black and non-Black candidates depended on those candidates' willingness to address issues of interest to Black citizens.

* * *

SAAC also played a role in the effort to incorporate Scotlandville into the city of Baton Rouge. In November of 1971, the City-Parish Council agreed to submit two voting issues to the residents of Scotlandville: first, a vote on incorporation; and second, a vote on reapportionment of the council.

Acie Belton and other Second Ward Voters League supporters championed the incorporation. But East Baton Rouge's consolidated plan of government, which had been adopted some twenty-five years earlier, prohibited additional incorporations in the parish. If parish voters approved the measure on February 1, 1972, then Scotlandville residents could subsequently vote on the issue of their own incorporation. Belton appeared before the council at its November meeting, claiming that the 23,992 people who lived in the community wanted the "barrier to be removed" that kept them from voting on incorporation. He said the reasons for and against incorporation would be thoroughly explained to area residents. Belton maintained that systemized growth could be achieved thorough incorporation. In response, one councilman said, "Scotlandville couldn't carry its own weight of providing services," while another said the proposal was "setting a precedent"—in other words, that if Scotlandville was incorporated into the city, other areas might seek to be incorporated as well.

An incorporated entity must not only provide essential services but also be able to raise sufficient revenues to cover the cost of those services. Belton maintained that, as initially proposed, the area to be incorporated had approximately $13 million in assessments, greater than the East Baton Rouge Parish municipalities of Zachary and Baker combined.

In February, the parish electorate voted against the proposed amendment to the city-parish plan of government that would have allowed the incorporation of Scotlandville and potentially other areas as well. Three years later, the issue arose again—this time insidiously rather than directly. Dewey Hayes, a Black member of the 1973 Constitutional Convention from East Baton Rouge Parish, who served on the Local and Parochial Government Committee, succeeded in getting that body to adopt a provision allowing new communities to be incorporated by petition.

Hayes's action, in effect, attempted to amend the city's plan of government without giving the parish residents a vote in the matter. If the provision was successfully inserted into the proposed new constitution, the other sixty-three parishes of the state could impose a new community on East Baton Rouge Parish even if citizens of the parish rejected that particular section or the constitution as a whole. Hayes's proposal made it into the "home rule" section of the proposed new state constitution, which forbade local government charters from prohibiting the incorporation of a city, town, or village. The East Baton Rouge Parish plan of government was the target of that provision of the home rule charters. It would allow Scotlandville—or any other population center of the parish—to incorporate.

By February 1974, some knowledgeable persons urged that the incorporation of Scotlandville be given a closer look. One such voice was that of Cleve Taylor, the mayor's director of intergovernmental relations, who cautioned that taxation resources had to be examined first. He noted that once an area became incorporated, it had to assume responsibility for its police protection, fire protection, garbage and sewer collection, and housing code programs. Streets and drainage were other major areas of cost.

By November 1974, the issue of incorporating the area of Scotlandville into a municipality had moved from mere study to implementation, buoyed by the new state constitution, which took effect on January 1, 1975. The initial draft of a study by Dr. Roosevelt Steptoe, then director of economic research at Southern University, indicated the incorporation of Scotlandville was economically feasible. That determination was mentioned by State Representative Richard Turnley at a November 12, 1974, press conference.

Steptoe's study predicted the operation of a Scotlandville government would cost about $1.25 million annually. Turnley, supported by SAAC members, thought the proposed city would be able to generate that amount. Proposed boundaries of the incorporation area were Airline Highway on the south, Plank Road on the east, Thomas Road on the north, and the Mississippi River on the west. Significant financial contributions were expected from such entities as Ryan Airport, Woolco Shopping Center, Southern University, and several industrial sites within these boundaries. Thus, the study concluded that the benefits of incorporation outweighed the burdens associated with incorporation.

But as soon as the incorporation of Scotlandville became a real possibility via the new state constitution, efforts began on behalf of some institutions located within the proposed city boundaries to instead annex those resources into the city of Baton Rouge. Within three weeks of the effective date of the new constitution, Ryan Airport and the Woolco (now North Park) Shopping Center were moving in the direction of annexation. On February 26, 1975, the City Council voted to annex the Woolco Shopping Center into the city of Baton Rouge and also set the stage for the annexation of Ryan Airport. On March 12, the City Council made the annexation of Ryan Airport official. Black leaders implied the council's actions were motivated by racism. With two of the largest revenue-producing entities no longer part of the proposed city of Scotlandville, the outlook for incorporation seemed bleak at best. Thoughts began to turn instead toward annexing the Scotlandville community into the city of Baton Rouge.

The residents of Scotlandville had two proposals before them: to incorporate as a separate municipality or to be annexed into the city of Baton Rouge. At this juncture, a serious separation developed between the Second Ward Voters League and SAAC. In our first forays into civic and political engagements, we were all members of the Second Ward Voters League. Now, the Second Ward was championing incorporation, while SAAC supported annexation.

By the latter part of July 1975, the incorporation efforts began to dissipate as almost all—90 percent—of the property owners in the Southern Heights subdivision announced their opposition to the incorporation, primarily because of the lack of a diversified tax base. On April 28, 1976, the City Council voted to allow the annexation of Southern Heights into the city of Baton Rouge. Two weeks later the council met again but refused to reconsider the annexation.

The Southern Heights annexation remained in limbo because of a temporary restraining order. District Judge Melvin Shortess dissolved the order on May 21, 1976, but he did not issue a final ruling that the annexation was proper until March 22, 1977. Also pertinent was a petition of annexation by the Black residents of the Banks, Woodaire, and Airline Terrace subdivisions, which had been certified by the assessor's office. The City

Council annexed the Banks-Woodaire area into the city of Baton Rouge on December 22, 1976. The annexation of those subdivisions into Baton Rouge further dimmed the Scotlandville incorporation efforts.

The Second Ward Voters League promoted the advantages of incorporation as: (1) control by the Black community of its tax funds; (2) improved employment and economic conditions for residents, due to the hiring of local government employees and the enforcement of policies that required Scotlandville residents be hired for new construction jobs; and (3) increased political power, with officials elected citywide. Yet area residents saw how difficult it was for Blacks to gain office and felt removed from decision-making processes. SAAC and others (including the Public Affairs Research Council) concentrated on the fact that incorporation meant that the costs involved had to be faced, understood, and accounted for.

On July 11, 1977, city-parish official Cleve Taylor and parish Councilman Jewel J. Newman informed attendees at a Southern University seminar on affirmative action hiring programs that "Scotlandville could not function at this time as a separate community because it could not generate the revenues needed to fund and operate a viable government." The City Council held a public hearing on October 11, 1978, to discuss a petition by many of the residents in the Scotlandville area concerning annexation into the city limits of Baton Rouge. SAAC strongly supported annexation, as did several council members and Mayor-President Woody Dumas. The council approved the annexation of most of Scotlandville on October 25, 1978, but it did not become effective until the beginning of 1979 due to a waiting period required by law.

Another event of concern to SAAC was the closing of the Food Town Supermarket & Ethical Pharmacy, located at 7850 Scenic Highway, which took place in early 1971. A number of us connected to the CAI Neighborhood Service Center joined with other area leaders in an attempt to keep the supermarket open. Forming the Scotlandville Cooperative of Progressive Entrepreneurs (SCOPE), we were able to continue operation of the supermarket for nearly a year. Because residents failed to shop at the store in sufficient numbers to generate adequate revenue for operations and provide some profits, the supermarket closed at the end of 1971.

Determined to fill the void created by the supermarket's closure, the leaders of SCOPE decided to convert the grocery store/pharmacy into a food cooperative. Thankfully, the Community Advancement Board of Directors provided the $25,000 grant needed to start the Scotlandville Cooperative. The advantage of the cooperative was that members could buy groceries at a very low markup. Only the actual cost of operating the store would be added to the prices, since the cooperative was a nonprofit organization.

To keep operating costs to a minimum, the number of employees ranged between one and three, and the store moved from the Food Town location to a smaller building on Scenic Highway at Sparrow Street, almost directly across from Camphor Memorial United Methodist Church. SCOPE's membership committee set a goal of five hundred low-income families to be part of the cooperative.

Yet the cooperative was not limited to one economic group or area. Families that were not classified as low income were strongly urged to shop at the cooperative store and to join as members; members could save 5 percent on food and 6 percent on nonedibles. Higher-income community members were asked to buy two or more memberships and donate one to a family of lower income.

At first, the plan was to reach the 500-member goal by July 27, 1972, and open the store on August 1. At a membership meeting on August 23, however, supporters learned that just 338 families had thus far paid the $6 membership fee. Because the drive recruiters were turning in names of additional member families at this meeting, SCOPE expected to reach its 500-family goal with no trouble; but a report the following day listed family memberships at only 420.

On August 30, the SCOPE board appointed Lillie Payne as the manager of the SCOPE Community Grocery Store in Scotlandville. Family memberships at that point totaled 465. Insurance had been arranged for, along with the bonding of Payne, and approximately $2,600 was on hand to finance the project. The store opened its doors in late September or early October 1972 after minor repairs to the building were made, the place was cleaned, a health inspection was done, and the store was stocked.

A grand opening celebration occurred on December 2, 1972. Store hours were from 7:30 a.m. to 7 p.m. Monday through Thursday, 7 a.m. to 8 p.m. Friday and Saturday, and 8 a.m. to noon on Sunday. The store had to become self-supporting within a year to stay open. But unfortunately, community residents found even more reasons not to shop at the cooperative than they had done at the resurrected Food Town Supermarket. Upper-income residents cited insufficient stock, limited parking, and difficult ingress and egress as reasons to stay away.

The first annual membership meeting of SCOPE was held on November 6, 1973, at Camphor Memorial United Methodist Church across from the cooperative store. As publicity chairman, I urged all cooperative members to attend to hear remarks and reports by board members James Wilson, Henry Allen, Ivory Ned, State Representative Richard Turnley, and T. T. Williams. We did our best to make the cooperative a success, but the store only lasted until about 1976.

The scarcity of supermarkets in underserved communities continues to be a problem to this day. On November 13, 2017, a Together Baton Rouge (TBR) rally held outside City Hall urged city-parish officials to spend more money to attract grocery stores to East Baton Rouge Parish. Residential areas more than a mile away from a grocery store are now referred to as "food deserts" and "grocery gaps." TBR, a faith-based community-organizing group in which I am an active participant, estimates that 17–23 percent of Baton Rouge's population lives in a "grocery gap," where people are not only far away from fresh food but also may lack the transportation they need to get to it. TBR has identified the three most significant grocery gaps in Scotlandville, Old South Baton Rouge, and the Florida Boulevard corridor.

Finally, there appear to be coordinated efforts among the various entities, such as TBR, Mayor-President Sharon Weston Broome, Broome's economic development departments, and citizens of the food desert areas, to entice major grocers to locate in underserved communities. Funding mechanisms are beginning to fall into place to attract grocers to these food desert areas. TBR believes there is a definite link between Baton Rouge's high obesity rates and the lack of access to fresh, nutritious food. Also, food at corner and convenience stores is usually more expensive than grocery store prices.

In 2019, the push for a grocery store in Scotlandville ramped up again with talks focused on the cooperative strategies it will take to make the longstanding dream a reality. Councilwoman Chauna Banks said she is interested in bringing in a grocery store that serves as an anchor to mixed development that offers entertainment and retail. Helping her in the efforts are TBR, Community Against Drugs and Violence, the mayor's office, and other community organizations.

Local residents saw a dream come true when a major supermarket opened on Florida Boulevard in January of 2024. When interviewed, the owner commented on the need and importance of the store to the area. Historically, there has been a perceived lack of spending power in the underserved community and badmouthing from real estate agents who paint North Baton Rouge as a high-crime area. Perhaps one day Scotlandville will have its grocery store too, with the help of the parties mentioned above, politicians, private sector investors, and the state of Louisiana.

Another significant event related to my SAAC involvement was my elected membership to the Democratic State Central Committee of Louisiana (DSCC). The DSCC is the governing body for Democratic Party activities and has sole responsibility for its affairs. All other Democratic organizations in the state of Louisiana are subject to the rules and governance of the DSCC. SAAC and its governing board recognized the critical importance of the DSCC in ensuring that elected and appointed officials truly represented the interests of Louisiana's Black citizens. Therefore, SAAC set out to elect DSCC members who would insist that these tenets remain at the center of all committee actions.

SAAC and its supporters had been pushing forward with election activities. As a well-functioning organization, SAAC was trusted by the community and looked to as a guide for political and civic activities. SAAC successfully got Jewel J. Newman (SAAC treasurer) elected to the City-Parish Council from Ward 2 in the general election held in November 1972. Newman took office on January 1, 1973. Then Johnnie A. Jones became the first Black elected to represent District 67 in South Baton Rouge. On August 8, 1975, Richard Turnley announced his intention to run for re-election to the House seat he had held since its creation four years earlier. At this point, I was serving as SAAC education coordinator. Some of the other SAAC members were Mitchell Albert, Myrtis Barnes, John E. Brown, Margery Hicks, Kenneth Joseph (vice chairman and chair of the Political Action Committee), Clayton Lewis, Allen J. Moye, and Harold Turner. Turnley won re-election to the District 63 House seat.

After the successful elections of Turnley and Newman, members of SAAC urged me to seek a seat on the Democratic State Central Committee. I offered myself as one of four candidates in the October 1975 election. When I announced my candidacy, I said, "Since this committee makes policy, arbitrates any disputes, and qualifies candidates, it is essential that persons reflecting a wide range of public interest and concern be a part of that decision making." I continued, "My experiences with the party and in campaign and election activities should serve me well in functioning at this level. I feel that I have the confidence of area residents that I both can and will express their concerns on the committee."

Seeking office seemed to me a natural extension of my civic involvement as a member of SAAC, the Anna T. Jordan Recreational Council, United Citizens for Community Action, the Scotlandville-Zion City Area Board of Community Advancement, Inc. (CAI) and its board of directors, the board of directors of the Scotlandville Food Cooperative, the East Baton Rouge Human Relations Council, the A. Philip Randolph Institute, and the Community Association for the Welfare of School Children. I was also president of the Park Vista Improvement Association.

I won a seat on the DSCC in November 1975, along with James H. "Chick" Edwards from District 29. I immediately became active in the group's affairs. I won re-election in 1979 and 1983. By January 1984, I served as the 4th vice chairman and a member of the Executive Committee with two other Blacks (Mary Wisham, secretary, and Walter Dumas, assistant legal counsel). I also served as a member of the Delegates Selection Committee for the 1984 Democratic National Convention.

In 1972, the Louisiana House District 63 Democratic Caucus selected me as an uncommitted delegate to the National Democratic Convention in San Francisco. There were a total of 12 uncommitted delegates, with 1 each for Hubert Humphrey, Shirley Chisolm, and George McGovern. All 12 were Black, including 5 women and 1 male under the age of thirty. The cancellation of the Louisiana presidential primary in 1984 resulted in the selection of delegates from each congressional district. Selection of 39 of the state's 69 delegates occurred by caucuses in the state's 39 senatorial districts. The remaining 30 delegates were selected from among party members and elected officials (i.e., members of Congress, the governor, mayors of large cities, statewide elected officials, state legislators, members of the Central Committee, and other state, parish, and party officials).

At the DSCC's January 15, 1984, meeting, I made a motion asking for a resolution objecting to suspending the presidential primary. On May 19, voters at about 90 polling places selected 39 delegates pledged to the presidential candidates. On June 2, the Central Committee chose the rest of the pledged delegates. Richard Turnley, Maxine Cormier, and I were elected by the 8th Congressional District Caucus as delegates pledged to Jesse Jackson. Jewel Newman was elected as an alternate.

I continued my active status in the DSCC and rose each year to the next level of vice chairmanship until I finally became first vice chairman in January 1987. At the July 1988 Democratic National Convention in Atlanta, I was a delegate again pledged to Jesse Jackson. By this time, demands on my time and efforts were piling up as a member and past president of the East Baton Rouge Parish School Board, so I did not seek re-election to the Central Committee. Though I was no longer actively involved in Central Committee affairs, I was concerned when Blacks gained leadership of the Democratic Party. Would they replace whites in a majority of positions, or would they be willing to share power? Without power sharing, would whites remain a part of the party? My thought, which I articulated to whoever would listen, was that—at the very least—power sharing was paramount or whites would abandon the party, and again we would be on the outside looking in.

That was the beginning of the migration of white Louisiana politicians to the Republican Party. Some Democrats left politics altogether, and some of their replacements were Republicans. Others switched parties even after their election as Democrats. The rebirth of the Republican Party was imminent.

A matter of concern to SAAC in the 1980s was the proposed relocation of the Scotlandville post office from its site on Scenic Highway to the southeast corner of Harding Boulevard and Plank Road in June 1987. When I first moved to Baton Rouge, there was a U.S. post office next to the Food Town Supermarket on Scenic Highway. It served between 25,000 and 40,000 residents living in the Scotlandville community.

According to the Postal Service, the proposed change of location came under consideration in 1982. Once we learned of these plans, SAAC and its leaders objected to the move. We wanted the post office to stay in Scotlandville, and we did not consider the corner of Harding Boulevard and Plank Road as being in Scotlandville. For context, the Louisa Street Post Office serving South Baton Rouge had also been closed, and there was no post office in Eden Park; those were two of the largest Black population centers in the Baton Rouge area.

Several people, including Metro Councilman Melvin "Kip" Holden, sought to label our objection as "personal business interest" since State Senator Richard Turnley, former Southern University chancellor Roosevelt Steptoe, State Representative Joseph Delpit, I, in my capacity as a member of the school board, and others owned the building housing the post office and grocery store. But we had not invested in the building because the post office was there. We did so to improve the economic environment of the Scotlandville area. We had invested in the building some fifteen years earlier, around 1972, after the closure of the Food Town grocery store. We had hoped to replace Food Town with a similar grocery store and put money back into the Scotlandville community.

State Senator Turnley (D-Baton Rouge) temporarily halted the move at the request of SAAC and some community members. He contacted the Louisiana congressional delegation and U.S. Representative Mickey Leland (D-Texas), who was the chairman of the House Committee on Postal Operations and Services. Unfortunately, when Senator Turnley lost his bid for re-election to Cleo Fields that fall, the post office was moved to 7980 Plank Road.

Postal officials said their plan to move the post office called for transforming the government-managed Scotlandville branch office into a "contract station," which would have allowed a private vendor to provide customer services there under a government contract. Today, there is no post office in Scotlandville at all, not even the promised contract station. Another viable economic entity vacated the Scotlandville community.

The year 1987 was an exciting one for SAAC and its supporters, as we learned of the possible removal of Dr. Joffre T. Whisenton from the office of president of the Southern University system. We had received word that input from the larger community was being sought on potential replacements. Several names arose. One in particular, however, brought almost unanimous agreement among members of SAAC present at the meeting: Dr. Dolores Spikes, chancellor of Southern University at New Orleans (SUNO).

Those speaking on Dr. Spikes's behalf pointed to her outstanding service in the university community. She had helped to form the Faculty Senate at SUBR in the 1970s, she had served as the Senate president in 1978, and she had served as the executive vice chancellor and vice chancellor for academic affairs at SUBR during the 1980s. When she was appointed chancellor of SUNO in July 1987, she became the first woman in Louisiana to head a public college or university.

By unanimous consent, SAAC submitted the name of Dr. Spikes for consideration. There is no way of knowing how many others may have made the same recommendation, but a great deal of support coalesced around what we had proposed, and we believe SAAC played a part as a creditable political and community organization. We presented Dr.

Spikes's stellar qualities to everyone who would listen. SAAC member and SU Board of Supervisors member Robert L. Jones carried the heavy load when articulating her qualifications to the board.

The Southern University Board of Supervisors agreed with our position and appointed Dolores R. Spikes as system president and interim chancellor of the Baton Rouge campus in 1988. Now Dr. Spikes had achieved not one but two Louisiana firsts: a woman as the head of a Louisiana college and a woman as the president of a multi-campus Louisiana higher education system. Dr. Spikes was also one of the few female college system heads nationally. She was a trailblazing giant in the field of higher education, both in Louisiana and the nation.

Seeing Dr. Spikes advance up the chain of higher education was particularly gratifying to me. For many years she had been my colleague at SUBR; we worked closely together to form the Faculty Senate. I also knew her as a neighbor. We lived in the same subdivision in Scotlandville. I knew her family members. Much of my interaction with her family occurred through my relationship with her husband, Hermon. Both of us were political novices and crossed paths while we sought election to several offices.

Though we were both college professors and neighbors and formality was not required, I routinely referred to her or addressed her as Dr. Spikes. I did this out of the tremendous respect I held for her. She was down-to-earth, straightforward, honest, and had a wonderful personality. People like that usually win me over every time. It causes me great pain when I walk by her former home, now vacant, because it reminds me that she, her husband, and her daughter have all passed away.

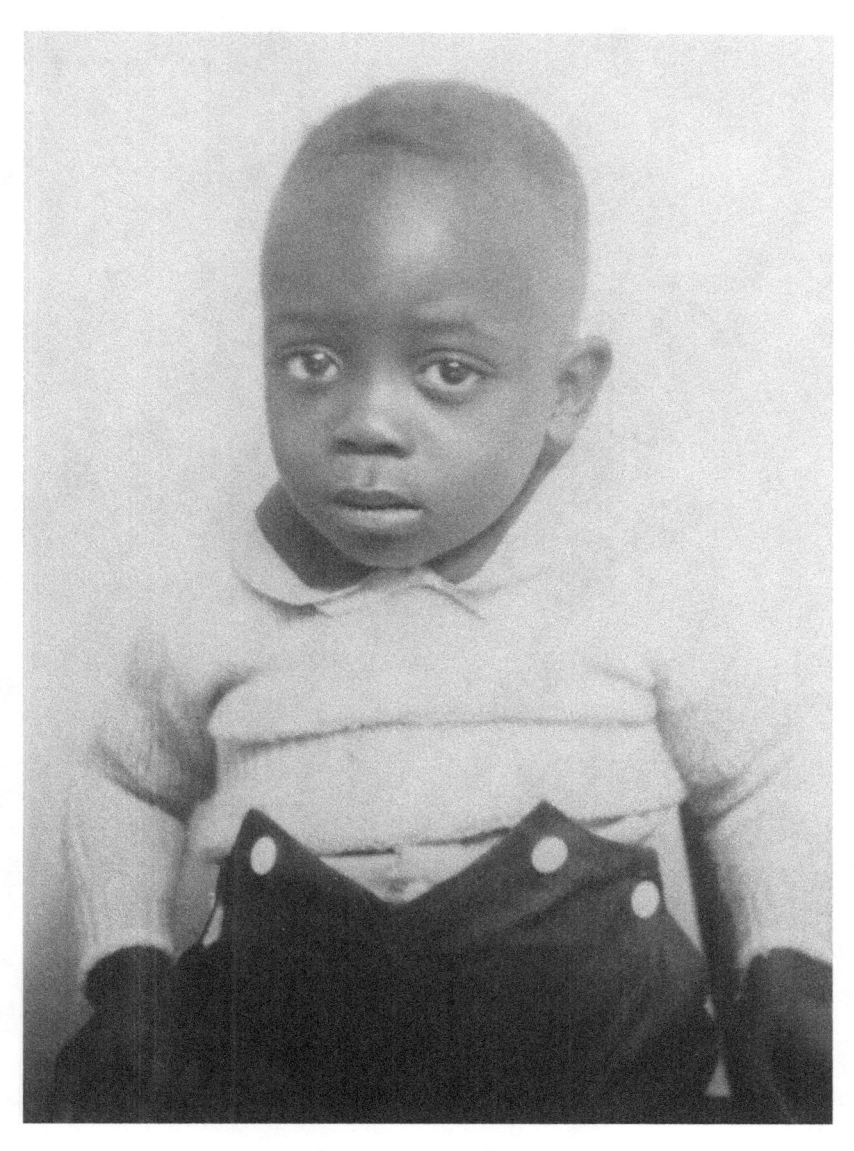

Baby Press, age unknown.
(Photo courtesy of the author)

Robinson as a young man, about 1962–63.
(Photo courtesy of the author)

Robinson addressing issues at a March 29, 1972, community meeting. (*Advocate* File Photo)

Robinson announces first run for school board seat, June 14, 1972. (*Advocate* File Photo)

Robinson elected chairman of the Baton Rouge Legal Aid Society. *Left to right:* Etta Kay Hearn, Treasurer; Robinson; and Doretha Rose, Secretary. (*Advocate* File Photo)

School board member Robinson studies preliminary racial mixing plan at board meeting. At Robinson's right is board member Sarah Edwina Prescott. (*Advocate* File Photo)

Robinson confers with board member Michael McCleary during desegregation discussions about whether Scotlandville High School should remain a comprehensive school with add-on magnets. (*Advocate* File Photo)

First elected to the school board in September 1980, Robinson begins his second term in 1983. (*Advocate* File Photo)

Newly elected school board vice president Robinson confers with board member Jim Talbot on an issue discussed by the board at a regular meeting. (*Advocate* File Photo)

Robinson and board member Eva Legard discuss the proposed suspension and tenure hearing against Mary Wisham, principal of Banks Elementary School. (*Advocate* File Photo)

School board staff reorder officers' names on the voting board as Robinson assumes his seat as the first Black board president. (*Advocate* File Photo)

Board president Robinson talks with reporters after first joint NAACP and board meeting on desegregation. (*Advocate* File Photo)

Board president/judge Robinson issues warning to attorneys during the tenure hearing session of William Breda, principal of McKinley High School. *Left to right:* Breda attorney Robert Williams, Robinson, and school system attorney Robert Hammonds. (*Advocate* File Photo)

Board president Robinson asserts before the Baton Rouge Press Club that classroom instructors won't be affected by teacher layoffs in the parish school system due to an $8 million budget shortfall. (*Advocate* File Photo)

Robinson gets a photo opportunity with Governor Edwin W. Edwards.
(Photo courtesy of the author)

Chancellor Robinson presides at the May 12, 2002, Southern University at New Orleans commencement. (Photo courtesy of the author)

Spring commencement at Southern University at New Orleans, May 8, 2004.
Left to right: Congressman William Jefferson, Chancellor Robinson,
SU System President Leon Tarver II, and presidential candidate John Kerry.
(Photo courtesy of the author)

Robinson and wife Ruth Ann.
(Photo courtesy of the author)

CHAPTER 7

My Waltz with the Courts

Life has smiled on me. Luckily I was in the right place at the right time to be able to influence history. In 1983 Freddie Pitcher Jr. was elected as the first Black judge on the Baton Rouge City Court. I am proud to have been his campaign manager.

Representative Richard Turnley, elected state senator in 1983, initially asked me to work for Pitcher's campaign on behalf of himself, Representative Joseph Delpit, and others supporting Pitcher. They believed I could boost Pitcher's campaign in the Black community. I did not know Pitcher but had met his law partners, Edsel Cunningham and Donald Avery. After visiting Pitcher at his law office on Plank Road, I realized how much I liked what I heard and saw. I therefore agreed to serve as his campaign manager.

As campaigns go, hard work and finances are always vital ingredients. Pitcher built a tremendously effective campaign organization and won the special election on March 26, 1983, to fill the 5½ years remaining in the term of Judge L. J. Hymel, who left the city court bench to become a district judge. At the time, Pitcher was thirty-seven years old and a graduate of the Southern University School of Law.

The Black church played a pivotal role in making Pitcher the first Black person elected as a judge in the city of Baton Rouge. Our campaign message extolled Pitcher's qualifications, emphasizing his temporary service as a judge, his tenure as a prosecutor, and his experience representing clients in civil and criminal cases.

Pitcher was a man of great talent. After four years of handling misdemeanor and small claims cases in the Baton Rouge City Court and three months as a district judge ad hoc, he wanted to expand his judicial influence by moving up to the 19th Judicial District Court. On November 21, 1987, that desire became a reality when Judge Pitcher bested assistant district attorney Prem Burns to become the first Black judge chosen for a district court seat in Baton Rouge. In 1992, the team of Pitcher and Robinson ran unopposed for the Louisiana First Circuit Court of Appeal.

Over many years of friendship and observation, I have developed a special respect for Judge Pitcher. We have a lot in common. We both grew up living in predominantly Black neighborhoods where we had to do without, I on a sharecropper's farm in South Carolina and Pitcher in the Valley Park neighborhood of Baton Rouge. Like my friend, whose industrious parents inspired him to be the best he could possibly be, I thank my hardworking parents who made it possible for me to be something better than a sharecropper. Simply because we were Black, we had to fight to accomplish things that we were capable of; otherwise, opportunities would never present themselves.

An incredibly special shout-out goes to Judge Freddie Pitcher Jr., my friend and fellow history maker.

Of the many concerns in Black communities for representation among our elected officials, the East Baton Rouge Parish School Board was high on the priority list and ripe for change.

On March 7, 1972, representing SAAC, I presented a single-member district plan for the school board to the Baton Rouge Ministerial Association and strongly urged its support of the plan. At the time, the school board used a multi-member election method, where all members ran at large within the ward in which they lived. There were three wards in East Baton Rouge Parish. Ward 1 was the city of Baton Rouge, Ward 2 was the area north of Florida Boulevard, and Ward 3 was the eastern part of the parish. More than once, election results demonstrated that Black candidates running ward-wide could not win the support of the political establishment or enough white voters to be successful.

These issues were keenly in play in October 1970, when Acie J. Belton sought support from the parish Democratic Committee for his candidacy for election to the East Baton Rouge Parish School Board. Belton was a political leader from Scotlandville and head of the Second Ward Voters League, in which many of us were members. He was well known throughout the city and parish. In an apparent compromise move, instead of supporting Belton's candidacy, the committee decided to support all Democratic nominees, opposed or unopposed, in the November 3 election. Belton was the only candidate who had opposition.

Turnley (of Ward 2 and the only Black member of the committee) and Sam Livors (chairman of the South Baton Rouge Advisory Committee, a predominantly Black political group) strongly urged the committee to support Belton's candidacy, both monetarily and otherwise. Livors went even further, telling the committee, "We need to get away from this wishy-washy Democrat-today, Republican-tomorrow business. I am begging you to do something for the Democratic nominee in Ward 2." His words had no effect. Belton lost the November 3 general election to Republican J. Clyde Geddes, who became the first Republican to gain a school board seat in recent history.

In my presentation to the Ministerial Association two years later, I pointed out that "the greatest concern in the Black communities in East Baton Rouge Parish is the exclusion of Blacks from the bodies that make decisions, and too often Blacks don't know about decisions until they appear in the newspapers." I also pointed out that there were 25,500 Black children in the parish, and "we have no voice in what happens to them. Single-member districts would help solve the problem because Blacks would have a clear majority of votes in one of the Ward 2 and one of the Ward 1 districts, and about a 50–50 split in another of the Ward 1 districts, with a strong voice in another Ward 2 district. We could have three Blacks on the school board, but now there are none." The Ministerial Association suspended its rules and voted 16 to 2, with 3 abstentions, to support the single-member district plan.

Belton and I, along with other prominent members of Black communities in East Baton Rouge Parish, continued our appeal to the school board to have single-member districts for school board elections. I reminded the board members that they had a moral and constitutional obligation to reapportion so that Black people could win election to the board. I reminded the board members that in the "fifties and sixties, Black people felt the lines of communication with whites were cut off, so they used confrontation-type tactics. But now, Blacks want to work within the democratic system, but if they are not allowed to, there may be a revival of the tactics of the earlier civil rights period." The school board said little about the revamp and took no action.

On May 19, 1972, I, along with Dr. D'Orsay Bryant, the Reverend H. P. Green, and Acie J. Belton, filed a class action suit against the East Baton Rouge Parish School Board, the East Baton Rouge Parish Democratic Executive Committee, the Board of Supervisors of Elections for East Baton Rouge, Registrar of Voters Mildred C. Bankston, and Secretary of State Wade O. Martin. The suit put forth the argument that "the [School] Board's present system of at-large representation violated the plaintiffs' rights by diluting the voting strength of Negroes and effectively denying them an opportunity to elect a member."

An amended petition later pointed out that the U.S. Justice Department had approved the apportioning of the city-parish council into twelve single-member districts. (Approval of the city-parish council plan came after we filed our suit.) Our amended petition said that, as an example of the potential impact of single-member districts for the school board, the council's reapportionment plan "virtually assured Negroes representation on the City-Parish Council" from the three large concentrations of Blacks in the parish, namely Scotlandville, the Eden Park and "Lake" areas, and South Baton Rouge. Judge E. Gordon West eventually dismissed the suit, saying he felt the plaintiffs did not show that Black voting strength had been diluted.

For the September 30, 1972, ward-wide school board election, I ran against J. O. Claudel in Ward 2—a new seat. Claudel beat me by 253 votes. I entered the school board race for a second time on August 14, 1976, the lone challenger to Claudel in Ward 2. I lost the ward-wide election to Claudel by 1,760 votes. Clara Mae Wells, a Black woman, failed in her bid for election to the school board from Ward 1. In all, I ran for a seat on the school board eight times, and I had at least one opponent in six of those races.

Between the 1972 and 1976 races, the death of Melvin "Coach" Geller in 1973 created a vacancy on the school board. On May 22, Governor Edwin Edwards appointed Lawrence E. Moch Sr., an Alpha Phi Alpha fraternity brother, to fill the vacancy. The first Black on the board, Moch served until a special election the following year to fill the remainder of Geller's Ward 1 term. In September, Moch lost his ward-wide runoff bid to white resident Herbert E. (Hots) Aull.

Moch was well qualified. He held a bachelor of science degree from Wiley College in Marshall, Texas, with further studies at both Southern University and Springfield College in Massachusetts. His career included positions as a certified director of the Young Men's Christian Association (YMCA) of North America; as an executive director of the Asheville, North Carolina, and Baton Rouge YMCAs; and as director of the Smith-Brown Memorial Union at Southern University. He was well known for his broad community involvement, both socially and politically. Aull was a real estate dealer who campaigned for neighborhood schools and against busing for "racial balance." White voters outnumbered the Black voters in Ward 1. Moch lost the race 55 percent to 45 percent.

It was clear beyond a shadow of a doubt that Black candidates could not win a ward-wide election for the school board, and I was not the only one convinced of that fact. On October 10, 1974, Lawrence Moch, George Eames, and I filed suit against the board to advocate for single-member districts, arguing that the multi-member ward system of elections violated Section 2 of the Voting Rights Act of 1965 and the Fourteenth and Fifteenth Amendments to the United States Constitution. This was the second attempt in a federal court by Black residents of the parish to have the school board elected by districts, similar to the city-parish district plan. Our suit was the third filed against the then-apportionment plan adopted by the board in 1971, which created one additional seat in Ward 2, bringing the total number of seats on the board to 12. Under the board's plan, there would have been seven seats in Ward 1, three in Ward 2, and two in Ward 3. Election of all members continued at-large in their wards. Also, at that time, school board members served six-year terms, with the terms staggered so that a collective memory existed after each election.

Defendants in the case were the East Baton Rouge Parish School Board and its individual members; Superintendent Robert Aertker; the East Baton Rouge Parish Democratic Executive Committee and its individual members; and the Board of Supervisors of Elections for East Baton Rouge Parish and its members.

Other plaintiffs were Secretary of State Wade O. Martin and Governor Edwin Edwards. Strong support for the suit was demonstrated before the board by Black elected officials in East Baton Rouge, such as State Representatives Richard Turnley and Joseph Delpit and City Councilman Howard Marsellus. Biracial Committee members G. Leon Netterville and Acie Belton, as well as Brenda Nixon of the Inner-City School Council, also supported the effort.

Judge E. Gordon West also dismissed the 1974 suit, saying it involved the same issues and parties. That dismissal was appealed to the Fifth Circuit Court of Appeals in New Orleans, which in turn was followed by a lawsuit by the U.S. Justice Department contending that Black voting strength decreased under the multi-member ward election system. That lawsuit spurred a scheduled hearing by the Fifth Circuit Court for November 17, 1976.

Belton lost again in 1976 to white candidate Martial J. LaFleur.

At an August 16, 1979, forum for public input held by the school board, seventeen individuals addressed the board on reapportionment, including State Representatives Richard Turnley and Joseph Delpit, City Councilman Howard Marsellus, Biracial Committee members G. Leon Netterville and Acie Belton, myself, and Brenda Nixon of the Inner-City School Council. Each of these speakers told the board its reapportionment plan should create 12 single-member districts, cause no reduction in the size of the board, cause no dilution in the voting strength of Blacks, and make use of districts created for city and parish council seats. Representatives Turnley and Delpit said they pushed the reapportionment into law in the regular legislative session of 1977 because none of the board members would "take the football and run with it."

The prospect of a Fifth Circuit Court ruling against the board; the specter of the new law from the Louisiana state legislature requiring all state school boards to maintain four-year concurrent terms instead of staggered terms; possible pressure from the U.S. Justice Department; and ongoing negotiations between the board, the three of us who filed the suit, and the Justice Department finally led to an agreement to form three single-member school board districts in which Black citizens constituted a substantial majority of the population in May 1980.

On June 6, 1980, federal Judge John V. Parker issued a court order putting the consent judgment and decree into effect. The decree was an agreement between the school board, the U.S. Justice Department, and the Black plaintiffs. The law passed shortly after the signing of the consent decree. It required school boards to switch from staggered to concurrent terms as quickly as possible and no later than 1986. The board approved an interim twelve-seat, single-member district plan on July 31 that called for the election of only seven board members (four white members whose terms expired that year and three new Black members). They were to assume two-year terms on September 13 (or if need be, in runoffs on November 4). That process resulted in a fourteen-member board until the 1982 elections, when all twelve board seats would come from single-member districts for four-year terms. The terms of the other seven white board members did not expire until December 31, 1982.

An interesting sideline to these negotiations was attorney Walter Dumas's comments to the board. He said, "If we're to give up single-member districts in 1980, we should at least submit the names of the persons who'll be appointed to the board. You'll make the choice. We're giving up a lot trying to negotiate. We can't give up too much." At this point, I suggested to Attorney Dumas that three new districts were needed, not one or two, to avoid any contention between Scotlandville, Eden Park, and South Baton Rouge about the appointee(s). Valor ruled that day. Three election districts were the result, and competition between the three areas of the parish was averted.

Eva Legard (representing South Baton Rouge), Frank Millican (representing Eden Park), and I (representing the Scotlandville area) were candidates in the September 13 primary election. I was elected to the school board outright and thus became the first Black elected member of the East Baton Rouge Parish School Board.

In the November 3 runoff election, Legard ran against Clara Mae Wells in District 6, and Millican ran against Albert C. Odell in District 5. All were Black candidates. Legard and Millican gained election to the board. As single-member districts materialized, my assertions to the Ministerial Board back in 1972 were proved accurate: three Blacks were now elected members of the board.

Making her fifth try for a seat, Clara Mae Wells, Legard's runoff opponent, articulated the stakes: "It's important that Black people have someone to identify with within the schools. Blacks didn't vote in past runoffs sometimes because they couldn't vote for anyone Black. For many, many years we have voted for whites. It's time we had Blacks on the ballot so we can be elected."

Legard ultimately gained the board presidency on January 10, 1991. She never seemed comfortable in that role, specifically in regard to the controversies and tough decisions that she had to face; her response when a resolution was found was to say, "Thank you, Jesus." Millican never did seek the post of board president; I think that he knew that his antagonism toward other members would most likely make that impossible.

I had no intention of seeking a seat on the school board when I was pushing for the single-member districts. Once the consent decree became a reality, members of SAAC began encouraging me to run. I did not take the urging seriously. One day someone said to me, "Hey, there's nothing to being on the school board. They only meet once a month, and that's all there is to it."

Not knowing much about the board and its operations, that sounded good to me. Plus, I reckoned that I could positively impact Black students in the public school system to the point that they would have fewer problems passing my chemistry classes at Southern. I realized most students had difficulties with chemistry because of three factors: lack of good reading and listening skills, generally poor math skills, and inadequate study skills. I reasoned that fewer students would have difficulty succeeding in chemistry if I could improve those three things. That reasoning, buoyed by members of SAAC and community voices, ultimately convinced me that I should run for a seat on the board. Once on the board, I often thought about that "they only meet once a month, and that's all there is to it" pronouncement. Oh, how seriously incorrect that was.

With the returns from the September 13, 1980, election promulgated by the secretary of state's office by October 24, the board requested that the federal court permit me to take my seat early. Therefore, I took the oath of office on November 6, 1980, rather than on January 1, 1981, which was the traditional time.

After voting 10–1 (J. O. Claudel dissented), board members expressed their desire to have the elected Black members seated early to assist in the formulation of an integration plan for presentation in federal court by January 9, 1981, and to promote acceptance of desegregation in the Black communities. This matter dated back to the 1950s, when the school board started its fight against the desegregation of parish schools; it continued through the 1960s, when the board supported separate but equal education; and it still continued into the 1970s, when voluntary integration produced no integration of Black schools in the parish. The issue of integrating the parish schools remained unaddressed as 1980 rolled around.

By the same 10–1 vote, the board approved a companion resolution asking Judge Parker to change his court's reapportionment order so that when new board elections took place in 1982, all members would be elected to four-year concurrent terms rather than staggered terms of two, four, and six years.

Both Legard and Millican took the oath of office at the school board meeting on November 20, 1980. Three new board members took their oaths that day, since Joan Houghton, a white member elected on November 3, took hers as well. Houghton defeated incumbent board member

Randall Goodwin in the November 3 election, and the board thus operated with fifteen members until December 31.

After the consent decree of June 6, 1980, board member Wally W. Wells resigned from the board effective June 30, leaving the rest of his term unfilled until December 31, 1982. The board then consisted of the regular 11 members, Houghton, and the 3 Black members for a total of 15 members. In my opinion, Wells's retirement came about because his home was located in the newly created single-member District 5, which consisted of a majority of Black voters. Wells admitted that the district residents would want to elect a Black school board member.

When I was elected to the East Baton Rouge Parish School Board on September 13, 1980, there were the usual slaps on the back for running a successful campaign. However, I had no "special feelings" other than that a milestone had been reached for Blacks in the parish. There were no thoughts of being the first or of making history. SAAC had accomplished something that no other individual or organization had done: elected a Black person as a member of the EBR school board.

Four years later, when the board elected me as its first Black president, I viewed this as the normal ascension of the vice president to the presidential position—a pattern the board had followed for most of its recent history. I was pleased to have been chosen and looked forward to the opportunity to further represent my community. After about a thirty-minute delay to allow for the changing of the order of names on the voting board, the meeting proceeded as scheduled with me presiding and without celebration. Even then, I made no attempt to characterize my election as president as anything other than my right to move up according to board practice. Privately, it was another accomplishment.

Immediately after taking my school board seat on November 6, 1980, I became outspoken in board matters by recommending the appointment of a Black architectural firm to inspect Harding Elementary School, which had sustained $250,000 worth of damage in a fire. After some haranguing, the board approved my recommendation. Prior to this, the board had not allowed minority contractors to perform significant work for the school system.

I became immersed in the desegregation negotiations between the plaintiffs, the Department of Justice, and the board. Hours, days, weeks, and months passed as we tried to develop a plan. To be truthful, many of those efforts were a waste of time because the white board members did not want a plan that would benefit everyone. Due to the board's inability to devise a plan acceptable to a majority of its members, we found ourselves in federal court.

In an effort to come up with a plan potentially acceptable to a majority of both the Black and white communities, presiding Judge John V. Parker recessed court negotiations for three days so that the school board could meet with its experts and come up with new ideas and approaches. Three days of intense negotiations between the parties, who were sequestered in his library, followed. The judge wanted us to be able to freely express our opinions without fear of retribution.

Judger Parker urged us to resist limiting our thinking to our single-member districts and to consider the good of the community. He also made it clear that he did not want to be the "Super-Superintendent" of the East Baton Rouge School System. If we could not devise an agreeable plan, he would have no choice but to issue one, and he assured us that in all likelihood we would not like his plan.

At times during those discussions it appeared that the parties were close to reaching a consensus. However, each time an agreement seemed within reach, the same two or three board members torpedoed it. Both leadership and courage were absent in the discussions, but a lack of courage was the greater deficiency. The white board members sought someone to blame for the inevitable attempt to desegregate the system, so they blamed Judge Parker. Unfortunately, no significant progress occurred, so on May 1, 1981, Judge Parker issued his desegregation plan. It primarily relied on race-based student assignments with mandatory attendance requirements, student busing, and magnet programs.

Much discussion between the board, the Department of Justice, the plaintiffs, and the judge followed that order for many years. I believe that

East Baton Rouge Parish is still not—and never has been—a unitary school system. To be unitary, the system had to eliminate racially identifiable schools, but the parties could never agree on what constituted such a school.

Instead of a given percentage of Black or white students in a school, other factors came into play: the physical location of the school and whether it was in an entirely Black or white neighborhood; whether the school had a Black or white history; and whether the principal and assistant principal were Black or white. The school board refused to apply any method of desegregation other than limited modification of attendance zones and contiguous pairing.

The East Baton Rouge school system desegregation plan was doomed from the start. The real problem was that some people did not want desegregation, and if they didn't like it, they didn't want to bus, regardless of busing's assets or liabilities. Immediately, several anti-desegregation efforts took place. I remember a well-known city councilman, George Dabbs, pronouncing publicly on TV after Judge Parker's order: "It ain't going to happen."

Black children boarded the buses and went to formerly all-white schools as called for by the desegregation plan, but most white students refused to be bused to or attend formerly all-Black schools. White communities established private academies for white students only and misused school system guidelines for student assignments. In other words, white students ignored assignments to formerly all-Black schools, instead attending other schools in the parish and surrounding parishes.

With white support for Dabbs's "ain't gonna happen" position and the subsequent drain of white students from the system, desegregation didn't have a snowball's chance in hell of success.

A note on terminology: During the early civil rights movement, the terms *integration* and *desegregation* were used interchangeably, but they are not the same. Integration involves combining actions or uniting people from different races to build a system affording people equal rights. Desegregation refers to the dismantling or tearing down of a racially separated system. The civil rights movement's take was that the racially segregated system was already established and needed to be torn down. Once that system was gone, everyone, regardless of race, would have the same rights. Thus, desegregation became the preferred term.

The school board tried several times to have the federal court consider new desegregation plans. By January 1987, the board was attempting to respond to two years of drum-beating discontent over busing by pulling and tugging at the 1981 federal court-ordered desegregation plan, seeking to reshape it into something that lessened busing and promoted a more neighborhood-centric approach.

Desegregation, the amount of busing needed to make it happen, and how the board handled the 1981 court-ordered mixing plan had all been consistently criticized by whites. As time went on, a growing number of Blacks were also challenging the way the board handled the plan, questioning the benefits of busing to Black students. A central issue in the controversy was the lack of trust in the board and system administrators by those who had supported busing since its implementation in the 1981–82 school year.

Charles Lussier, news editor of the *Baton Rouge Advocate*, outlined the historical path of desegregation in the parish school system. He pointed out that around the close of the 1960s, only 13 percent of the parish's Black children were enrolled at schools with white children. In the 1970–71 school year, 86 percent of the parish's Black children were enrolled with white children, but only in formerly all-white schools. Lussier further stated that of the 102 schools in the public system at the time, only 19 remained all Black or all white. Most of those were attended by Blacks only, although the number was half of what it had been the previous year. Children soon began re-sorting themselves on their campuses, and some families moved elsewhere in the parish or into neighboring parishes to maintain their personal status quo.

When the courts ordered desegregation, those in fierce opposition decided to start their own schools instead of integrating the public schools. As a result, private schools popped up all over the state, enrolling thousands of white students. These efforts to form separatist schools received aid from the state of Louisiana, which set aside $10 million to help pay the salaries of teachers at these new segregationist academies.

During this transition period, many Black high schools, in East Baton Rouge Parish and elsewhere in Louisiana—which were formerly pillars of their communities—underwent significant changes. Some were converted into junior highs, others were closed, and still others were demolished altogether. Many of their best teachers were transferred to white schools in an effort to achieve court-ordered faculty ratios.

Further erosion of the East Baton Rouge Parish School System (EBRPSS) occurred in 1995, when the city of Baker began pressing to pull out and form its own school system. I knew then that Baker's action was a precursor to the physical dismantling of EBRPSS. I made it known that I believed that if Baker left, Zachary would go too, as would Central, and finally southeastern Baton Rouge. The EBRPSS no longer includes three of those communities, and as of this writing, southeastern Baton Rouge is seeking to follow suit.

By 2020, white students made up 11 percent of the enrollment in East Baton Rouge Parish public schools, and in 2019, for the first time, Hispanic students outnumbered whites. Baton Rouge had its chance to get desegregation right but failed to do so. So did the plaintiffs, such as the NAACP, who could and should have fought for equal resources instead of Black and white kids in the same classrooms—a recommendation I made in 1970 at a Baton Rouge Magnet High School meeting. (I had also suggested we begin the process with students in the first grade; instead, the process was begun with 12th graders, which I believe was intentionally designed to produce negative results.)

We, as Blacks, had better-educated teachers (many with master's degrees or master's degrees plus thirty hours), strong family units, and a burning desire to improve our livelihoods. Desegregation destroyed those assets when our best teachers were taken from the Black schools and sent to white schools, when our best students got assigned to the white schools, and when many of our facilities were closed or converted to less-demanding educational institutions under duress. Most of our leaders were demoted to relatively unimportant positions. Some experienced disrespect and dehumanization. In my estimation, desegregation has failed to improve Black students' lives and achievements, and integration was never a real possibility. In my mind, desegregation was the worst thing to happen to Black people since slavery. The question we must answer today is whether or not Black Americans are still effectively in slavery—just not the kind that we normally think about.

Had my 1970 recommendation been adopted, I believe the East Baton Rouge Parish school system would be better off than it is today. Another plausible solution: had the school board actually implemented special programs (magnets desired by white students) as they should have at predominantly Black schools, I firmly believe that white students would have voluntarily sought them out and self-integrated. All of that was but a faded memory by 2022, as few schools of any kind under the control of the East Baton Rouge School Board have a substantial racially mixed student body. Public schools inside the city limits are predominantly Black or other minority, while private and suburban public schools are nearly all white. This fact means that the school system reflects, regrettably, a still divided community. Even though I spent more than twenty-two years on the school board trying to convince the white board members that Black folks had the same aspirations as white folks and deserved a fair chance to achieve them, equality never materialized. The fight continues, and there is no end in sight. We are still a long way from having equal opportunities to achieve the "American Dream."

I mentioned earlier that a fellow SUBR chemistry professor, Dr. Wilbur B. Clarke, became my ardent bowling partner. Here is a brief story about bowling.

Upon the signing of the 1964 Civil Rights Act, many southerners felt that the South had overcome its segregation struggles. Many whites and Blacks believed that the worst of the South's racial conflict was over, and a sense of optimism gripped the region. People assumed that everyone knew that the Civil Rights Act was the law of the land and that they would abide by it. A large part of the South did comply with the act, though, at the same time, civil rights organizations sought a cessation of demonstrations for a specified period and encouraged deliberate biracial efforts to reduce friction. Some people believed that voluntary desegregation of schools in some parts of the South demonstrated changing of attitudes and better cooperation between white and Black leaders.

In 1964 I was part of a small group of Baton Rouge area residents who pushed for the integration of local bowling alleys. Wilbur Clarke, my close associate at SUBR, had piqued my interest in learning to bowl. The only bowling alley available to Blacks was a small one in the university student union. We enjoyed bowling there, but the facility was small and manual racking of the pins was required, thus slowing down the game. There were two mechanized bowling alleys in Baton Rouge that had automatic racking of pins; they refused to allow Blacks to play. When we learned that President Lyndon Johnson had signed the Civil Rights Bill into law, several of us rushed to Plank Bowl, the closer of the two mechanized alleys, and requested to play on its lanes. We were flat-out denied.

We knew the response of the alley management would be negative, but we were determined to change that course. We pressed the issue for about six months, after which management relented and offered us the opportunity to bowl on the last two of the forty lanes in the establishment. A group of us accepted that arrangement for a few months and then began asking to bowl on any lane in the building. The woman managing the facility immediately rejected those requests, leading to verbal confrontations with those of us seeking broader access to bowling than lanes 39 and 40.

We had no idea that the new law did not specifically encompass a number of public establishments, including bowling alleys. I am not sure whether this alley management realized that or not, but it was never given as the reason for denying us the chance to bowl. More often than not, management told us that bowling leagues had reserved all the lanes. We knew that leagues bowled at night, and we argued that we should be able to use any lanes we desired when the leagues were not there. I found myself proffering that position many times, as Wilbur and I loved to bowl.

Plank Bowl's management determinedly denied our requests. But even as we were arguing with Plank, we discovered that Melrose Bowling Lanes' management was more lenient. Consequently, we readily drove the extra seven or eight miles to Melrose Bowl. Bowling at Melrose gave us the opportunity to form a mixed bowling league, comprised of both men and women, and to develop our skills. By early 1966, Blacks had formed the Bayou Strikers men's league, followed shortly thereafter by the Rougettes women's league.

On September 6, 1967, the U.S. Fifth Circuit Court of Appeals held that dance studios, bowling alleys, and certain amusement parks were not subject to the public accommodations section of the 1964 Civil Rights Act. That opinion originated from a suit by Patricia B. Miller, on behalf of her children, against Amusement Enterprises, Inc., operators of Fun Fair Park of Baton Rouge. Fun Fair Park was refusing to serve Black children. My family and I visited Fun Fair Park many times after 1971.

In 1967, the Southern Bowling Congress (SBC) held a tournament in Baton Rouge. By that time, the Bayou Strikers had become an established league, bowling weekly like other leagues. My five-member team, consisting of Wilbur Clarke, Leo Paul, Thornton Rhodes, Ernest Simon, and myself, competed without incident. Following our SBC tournament appearance, Clarke and I made it a point to enter other competitions in other cities, both in and out of state. We bowled in the singles or the doubles group depending on the setup. Blacks formed several leagues that bowled religiously every week well into the 1990s. My bowling days ended in 1980, when I was elected to the East Baton Rouge Parish School Board.

Unfortunately, the Civil Rights Act was not the silver bullet people thought it would be. We are still fighting today to change white attitudes toward Blacks and their place in American society. In 2022, the struggles seemed to have become even stronger. On April 7, the school board voted 5 to 4, strictly along racial lines, to temporarily approve a nine-member redistricting plan that maintained a white majority on the board, despite pleas from the community for an 11-member or greater board with a majority of majority-minority districts. Not only is the voting population of the district majority Black, but the student enrollment is also close to 90 percent Black. These redistricting maneuverings are about maintaining white control of political processes, and those efforts are repeated in many states.

As I have said before: the more things change, the more they stay the same.

CHAPTER 8

Challenges, Challenges, Challenges

In September 1983, upon the death of then-Vice President Sarah Edwina Prescott, I was elected, 10–1, as the first Black vice president of the school board in a head-to-head contest with white board member Robert Crawford. Crawford had served on the board for several years before I arrived and felt that he should be vice president, particularly since the newly elected VP would be replacing another board member with longevity. But in my short time on the board, I had built good relationships with most of the members, and they appreciated my ability to work cooperatively.

Prescott was a person reasonably easy to like. She treated the Black members of the board with dignity and respect, as did her husband, James D. Prescott. During much of my tenure on the school board, James Prescott was the president of the Louisiana School Boards Association. I was in their home many times, and I worked closely with the association.

I believed that the working relationship between myself, as the board vice president, and Mike McCleary, its president, was solid and an asset to the board. Past board practice was that vice presidents automatically became presidents at the end of the president's term, and presidents always left office after a two-year stint. I did not expect to have to fight McCleary for the president's job in January 1985. But for reasons unknown to me and never adequately explained, McCleary decided he was not ready to give up the president's position.

CHALLENGES, CHALLENGES, CHALLENGES

McCleary's decision generated an added factor in the election process. Usually, the question before the board would have been, who will be the new president? But now the larger question before the board was whether McCleary should even be running.

On January 10, 1985, there was a loud round of applause from the audience when the school board voted 7–5 to elect me as its president. The vote ended one of the fiercest and most public battles for that position in recent history. Many kudos went to board member Sue Fowler for the courage she demonstrated in nominating me for president. I appreciated the seven board members who initially supported me for the post and the other four who switched their votes after the first count. I never held any animosity toward T. H. Montgomery for being the lone dissenting vote both in the 1983 vice president's election and the 1985 president's election.

I was very pleased that the board elected Robert Crawford as vice president, thus restoring its custom of electing its most senior member as vice president and having the vice president become the president after a two-year term. I realized the tremendous burden thrust on me as the first Black president of the East Baton Rouge Parish School Board, but I also welcomed the challenge.

Leading up to the election, there had been both public and private meetings between business leaders from the Black and white communities concerning the ramifications of my presidency on the local public school system. White students were already leaving the public school system, and questions kept coming as to whether my election as president would cause further white flight and whether I would be a help or a hindrance in dealings with the NAACP in court battles over school desegregation.

Over time, I believe I demonstrated that I could be board president and help move the system forward. I always had a realistic view of the situation and knew I was under the microscope much more than any president of the board before me had been. I believe that had I not been president, direct discussions between the NAACP and the board would not have occurred. It was a challenging task to convince the NAACP, the plaintiffs in the desegregation suit, and the school board to ease their animosity toward each other, sit down together, and have a profound and respectful dialogue.

Those discussions set the stage for the ultimate agreement between the parties to end the 47-year-long desegregation suit (initially filed in 1956), although it took some 18 years (June 18, 2003) following my first election to the office of school board president and came a year after I resigned from the board to be chancellor at Southern University at New Orleans. I sincerely thank Beverly Vincent for her willingness to complete my four-year school board term for several months in 2002 and the board for accepting my replacement recommendation.

Interactions between the various parties, the public, and the media were often contentious. Attorneys were concerned about what legal parameters to set that would establish the groundwork for reaching a settlement; what degree of confidentiality was needed for them to be able to prepare litigation documents effectively; how to ensure the sufficiency of all legal aspects of any plan developed; how best to conduct discussions among the litigants; and how best to litigate on their clients' behalf. Unfortunately but predictably, the board was criticized for meeting privately with its lawyers, the lawyers for the plaintiffs, and several key school officials.

When I was asked about those meetings by the media, I expressed my belief that public bodies must have an opportunity to talk without having their ideas scrutinized before they are fully developed. Some thoughts are just that—thoughts—and deserve no further consideration. Others may require intense scrutiny before being seriously discussed. That's why state law allows public bodies to meet in private under certain circumstances—so they can have honest and true discussions. You cannot have open meetings about a lawsuit and simultaneously protect the interests of the participants.

At some point, however, the public must be involved in the process, as was the case with our school board. Fortunately, the court shared the board's opinion with respect to the need to meet privately and in some cases issued gag orders, which prevented the parties from discussing evolving documents.

Loads of school board money were spent "fighting" desegregation of the system in the form of attorneys' fees; legal preparations and court appearances; and constructing various plans for submission to the board, plaintiffs, and the court, plus related expenses. One can only wonder how much spending occurred. I am not aware of any efforts to capture that information; if captured, that information was not shared with the board in any organized fashion. The complexity of developing a desegregation plan was enormous and required a mountain of time and money.

A workable plan that successfully integrated a school system required one crucial ingredient: a sincere desire to achieve the stated goal. Unfortunately, neither the school board nor the parish's white politicians and residents had such a desire. Judge Parker, who inherited this case on September 27, 1979, saw this suit as I did. In 2001, he expressed extreme frustration with the school board and withdrew from the case with this comment: "This School Board and its lawyers would still rather litigate than desegregate." The case eventually was assigned to U.S. District Judge James Brady.

Desegregation was only one of the many issues that faced the school board, and nearly all of them required making tough decisions. There were issues regarding a zero-tolerance policy toward fighting; mandatory uniform policies in elementary schools; academic programs aimed at improving test scores; members' respect for each other and their ability to "disagree agreeably"; transportation and school starting/ending times; the gifted program; a 1998 tax plan; the breakup of the parish's school system; and the emerging threat of charter schools.

The lack of parish residents' commitment to the desegregation plan was profoundly demonstrated by their failure to approve critically needed school construction funds for the decades between 1969 and 1998. The conflict about racial desegregation overshadowed every other issue—in particular, the need to provide more funds for the schools. Thankfully, the community finally came to the school system's rescue in the form of a dedicated one-cent sales tax in 1998 following the board's cessation of forced busing in 1996. The system still had decades of neglect to overcome, however, and the tax was reapproved in 2003, 2008, and 2018.

Meanwhile, student enrollments in Baton Rouge public schools have steadily decreased over the years. There were 64,079 students enrolled in 1981–82 (60/40 white/Black), 59,000 in 1990–91 (45/55 white/Black),

58,328 in 1995–96 (39/61 white/Black), 54,848 in 1999–2000 (33/67 white/Black), and only 43,000 in 2010–11 (18/82 white/Black). The current system website states that 41,300 students are served. There is no mention of the racial breakdown of students, but I surmise that the enrollment of Blacks and other people of color exceeds 90 percent. How much longer will the majority-white public in Baton Rouge be willing to fund a "Black school system"?

Among the pressures being applied to dismantle the public education system are those exerted by the charter school movement. A letter to the editor in the September 17, 2020, issue of the *Advocate* quoted the then-vice president of the EBR school board as saying that kids had a "slim to none" chance of getting a quality education if they did not attend a magnet school or a charter school. This individual appears to have given up on our non-magnet and non-charter schools, yet he serves on the board that determines the quality of education available to local students. In fact, as of 2024, a majority (8–1) of the sitting school board members, including two Black members, are pro-charter. I find that to be ironic.

In 2021, there were twenty-nine charter schools in the Baton Rouge area, enrolling approximately 11,000 students. Fourteen of those schools received approval from the local board, but fifteen others gained approval from the State Board of Elementary and Secondary Education (BESE) after the local board rejected them. One can only speculate that the money interests are aligned, to the detriment of our public school system.

The State of Louisiana instituted public school letter grades in 2011 (replacing the previous system of stars), but now, a little more than a decade later, BESE wants to shelve them. The monetary drain on the public school system is substantial and ever increasing. On March 1, 2022, at a "solutions summit," the director of education and workforce development for the Louisiana Association of Business and Industry praised the push to revamp state public schools by allowing students to leave their classrooms and take their state portion of annual aid with them. Another topic at the summit was education savings accounts (ESAs), which would give families access to their annual state education aid —around $5,500 per student—to help pay for a private school, tutors, technology, or other options (perhaps even to supplement vouchers). The Louisiana state superintendent of education has strongly and publicly endorsed ESAs, which would further undermine the stability of the public education funding system. The future of the East Baton Rouge public school system indeed looks bleak.

Of all the challenges I faced while serving as president of the school board, perhaps the greatest was my role as a presiding officer, with judicial responsibilities, in the tenure hearing of William Breda, principal of historically Black McKinley High School. Based on allegations by several white female teachers and students, Superintendent Raymond Arveson's administration accused Breda, a Black man, of sixteen charges of incompetence and willful neglect of duty. Several weeks of investigations by the administration followed. At first, the superintendent maintained that he did not have enough information to initiate a hearing. Following school board member Jim Talbot's request for information about Breda, however, Arveson changed his mind: now he had enough.

The board later approved calling for a tenure hearing for the principal. The vote, along racial lines, was 9 to 3. A request to forgive the principal of all charges failed by the same 9 to 3 vote. School boards in Louisiana cannot fire or otherwise affect an employee's tenure without first making a list of charges available to the employee and holding a hearing to answer the charges. The hearing may be public or private, at the option of the employee. Breda chose a public hearing. It seemed as if the intent was to fire him. Breda filed suit requesting an injunction to block the July 8, 1986, tenure hearing, but District Judge William Brown rejected the motion for injunctive relief. Judge Brown said there was no evidence that Breda could not receive a fair hearing before the board.

School board member Jim Talbot first brought the issue to the administration, supposedly based on signed statements from both teachers and students. When the specific charges became known, the three Black board members concluded that the situation did not warrant anything beyond administrative attention. The complaints appeared to be simply teacher gripes, nothing more.

In the thirty-three years that Breda served the parish school system, no known disciplinary actions had been taken against him. He was considered to be one of the top principals, of any race, in the system. Teachers, parents, and students admired him and regarded him as a true mentor. Following desegregation in 1981, however, things changed. In the vast majority of cases, when southern school districts underwent desegregation, Black administrators experienced demotion, reassignment, and sometimes even lost their jobs when schools mixed populations. But during desegregation, Breda was kept on as the principal of McKinley while white teachers and students were assigned to the school.

I believe that the charges against Breda arose for two reasons. First, white female teachers did not like answering to a Black administrator, or perhaps others objected to the teachers' reporting to a strong Black principal. Second, Breda did something that no other principal had had the guts to do. He spoke out about the lack of enforcement of the system's school zone rules, noting, "The problem of students attending schools outside their assigned districts is widespread and is not limited to athletes."

It's possible that Talbot, then a candidate for the mayor of Baton Rouge, arranged the episode in an attempt to boost his campaign. Talbot wrote a letter to William Bradford Reynolds, head of the U.S. Justice Department's Civil Rights Division, seeking the reassignment of Attorney Franz Marshall because Marshall sat quietly at the defense table monitoring the proceedings during Breda's July 8, 1986, tenure hearing. Marshall represented the Justice Department in support of the plaintiffs in the East Baton Rouge Parish school desegregation case. Board member Frank Millican and I both wrote response letters stating that Talbot's accusations had no basis in fact. Marshall remained on the desegregation case and continued representing the Justice Department in the 47-year-old suit until 2003, when a consent decree ended the case action.

Louisiana tenure law mandates that the school board president sit as a judge. However, I also wanted to serve as the judge in the Breda tenure hearing to make sure that equitable rules governed the process and that he would receive as fair a hearing as possible under the circumstances. Allowing someone else to preside would have required the board to intervene on the matter and might have led to more acrimonious infighting between board members.

Several board members seemed to have formed negative opinions of Breda even before the scheduled hearing took place. Considerable controversy resulted from the hearing, expanding beyond the school board. The atmosphere in the hearing room was extremely tense. The attorneys in the case, Robert Hammonds for the school board and Robert Williams for Principal Breda, made my job harder than it should have been because they kept using legal terms and employed courtroom tactics, such as making constant objections and resorting to lengthy cross-examinations. I had to continually remind them that we were in a tenure hearing and not in a court of law, and that I was determined to make a decision that was right for all those involved.

I could not allow my personal feelings to interfere with what I deemed to be fair and proper. Sadly, I often needed to remind board member Frank Millican not to cross-examine witnesses. Millican referred to the proceedings as a "kangaroo court" and accused the white board members of being motivated by race when they pushed for the hearing. Some white board members attempted to override the chair when I ruled on objections.

Meanwhile, Talbot's feelings about the hearing and Breda seemed to be summed up by his reaction to a comment at the hearing by a McKinley teacher, who claimed to have seen Breda and other school officials eating at the school, despite a rule prohibiting food consumption outside the cafeteria and home economics areas. She maintained that he had been eating toast.

There was laughter from the audience following that remark, and Talbot complained about the "unfair hardship" teachers faced when testifying at the hearing sessions. He said, "I don't think it's proper for us to allow an audience reaction that is very favorable to Mr. Breda. Somebody needs to stand up and say enough is enough. Please give our teachers the respect they deserve or go home."

Tenure hearings can result in dismissal, exoneration, a reprimand, a suspension, a demotion, a transfer to another school, or a combination of two or more things. Allegations of racial bias made by the all-white group of teachers who submitted written complaints against Breda, who was Black, had drawn the attention of other segments of the community. Efforts were made to reach a compromise as the case moved through the tenure hearing process. The issue of race also created tension on the board, which was split along racial lines in the recurring 9 to 3 votes that moved the Breda case center stage. After four long and contentious hearing sessions, I recessed the hearings indefinitely on Monday, July 21, 1986, in order to make progress in slashing approximately $6 million from the board's budget.

On Friday, July 25, 1986, William Breda was at a quiet McKinley campus preparing for his eighteenth year as principal and wishing for another smooth opening day. It was hoped that the summer recess would have reduced the racial tensions generated over the embattled Black principal. Still, squabbles between the school board, the NAACP, and community officials over how to handle the case made that possibility remote. The Louisiana National Baptist Convention requested that the school board drop the sixteen charges against Breda, to no avail.

Intending to retire at the end of the 1985–86 school year, Breda changed his mind because of the tenure charges and hearings. At the time, the school board granted transfers to other schools in the district to teachers who testified against Breda during the tenure hearings. On August 27, 1986, Breda confirmed his plan to retire from the East Baton Rouge school system effective August 29. His retirement made the continuation of the tenure hearings moot and allowed the school board to get back to other system issues. But in my opinion, the hearings should never have taken place, and had Breda been white, they would not have.

Charlie Thomas Jr., the Black principal at Northeast High School, assumed the principalship at McKinley High on September 25, even though longtime assistant principal Clarence Jones and two others, who were also Black, applied for the job. Breda passed away in 2004 in Arizona, where he had lived for fourteen years.

The Breda saga and the desegregation plan were not the only issues that Black board members had to step up to handle. The three of us found ourselves immersed in dispute after dispute. Some white principals made it a point to take drastic action against Black teachers and other Black employees. Typically, the administrative structure handled such issues, but often there were efforts to summarily dismiss or demote Black employees for minor offenses, of which white employees were also guilty. It was common to find one, two, or all three of us Black board members at a school trying to mediate disciplinary actions taken against a Black employee by a white principal.

I still frequently come into contact with people who tell me how much they appreciated my help in those situations. Sometimes I remember my involvement; in most cases, however, I have no recollection of the situation. I appreciate hearing about being helpful to citizens no matter at what level or under what circumstances. Such direct involvement in day-to-day operations was not, and should not have been, part of our board service. Because the need arose, we got involved until such behavior subsided, which finally happened five to ten years later.

In January 1987, following my first stint as president of the board, Jim Talbot decided to break with the longstanding tradition of the vice president ascending to the presidency and challenged Robert Crawford for the position. He withdrew from the race on election day, and the board unanimously elected Crawford. Talbot subsequently served as board president from 1989–1990, and then he caught us all off guard by announcing his resignation from the board on July 11, 1991, with three and a half years left in his four-year term.

The local newspaper, the *Morning Advocate,* reported the news as follows: "School Board member Jim Talbot resigned from the board Thursday in a fashion typical of his nine years in office—by surprise and keeping his 11 colleagues off balance." Local NAACP president George Washington Eames reacted by saying, "Good. I think that Jim did East Baton Rouge Parish a disservice because I do not think he read the court order and never understood what his mission should have been." Eames was, of course, referring to the desegregation lawsuit. Talbot later described his nine years on the school board as a succession of pitched battles. The grind finally wore him down and probably kept him out of the political limelight.

An interesting side note to the Jim Talbot/Frank Millican saga is worth mentioning. Millican, a Black board member representing District 5, often clashed with Talbot over issues of race. On December 1, 1988, Millican, sitting next to me at a regularly scheduled board meeting, had just completed a rather long statement about the topic under discussion. As he finished talking and attempted to sit back in his chair, I heard a faint groan and turned to my right to see if he was okay. He was slumped over slightly, with his head against his upper chest. Knowing that his position was unnatural, I rushed to raise his head and loosen his tie. No matter how hard I tried, I was unable to do either, because his head was locked in the downward position.

As I struggled to assist him, other board members realized something was amiss and rushed to help. Millican was a big man, and it took three of us to get him out of his chair and onto the floor. Once on the floor, he was given mouth-to-mouth resuscitation, to no avail. When the paramedics arrived, it was too late. Millican had succumbed to a massive heart attack. But none other than Jim Talbot performed the mouth-to-mouth resuscitation.

In November 1994, a historic parish school board election ushered in nine new board members, all Republicans, and a return of three incumbents.

A brash young white Republican named Mike Branch was among the returning members. First elected in 1990 to represent District 11, Branch had defeated Gordon Hutchinson, who in 1987 replaced retired T. H. Montgomery after some forty years on the board. Hutchinson was realistic in his support for getting the school system released from the federal court busing order. Any knowledgeable person familiar with the school system and the desegregation case plaintiffs knew that single-race neighborhood schools were unlikely to return. Branch showed no such honesty and gave the citizens of District 11 hope that it might happen. Re-elected without opposition in 1994, Branch decried forced busing and maintained that he was fighting for neighborhood schools. He tapped into the wholesale resentment of the school system by the community of Central, arguing, "Nothing irritates me more than to hear people say we can't do anything about our situation. We can. If we want things to happen, we must make them happen."

That was Branch's way of putting a conservative spin on "power to the people"—power to the people who were "madder'n hell." He was giving the residents of District 11 an outlet for their frustration. He didn't have to actually deliver a neighborhood school. He just had to deliver a message.

One method he used to convey his message was to try to irritate, upset, throw off guard, or rattle me, as the president of the board, as well as the other board members. I assumed he wanted to show his constituents that he could control "that Black son-of-a-gun" who had the nerve to lead the board.

Organizations like school boards function best when they operate via reasonable and understandable rules of engagement. Compromise is critical. Very seldom does anyone engaged in the political process get everything they want. Branch demonstrated his alienation from the rest of the board even before taking office. He refused to attend a retreat of board members who would take office on January 1, 1995, citing a scheduling conflict. The retreat, held at the Asphodel Inn in Jackson, Louisiana, enabled the nine new board members and two incumbents to get to know, respect, and trust each other.

Branch would interrupt other board members while they had the floor. I constantly had to remind him that he was out of order. He knew that every member of the board wishing to be heard on a topic of discussion would be given an opportunity to speak, with the order determined by me, as board president. Nonetheless, he consistently spoke out of turn and raised points not germane to the issue under consideration. One can imagine the frustration of the board members and people in the audience when discussions were disrupted by his extraneous behavior or ideas. In essence, Branch's behavior could have been considered anti-establishment. He and his constituents maintained that he was simply bashing special interests.

Mike Branch's game plan became obvious when I and others learned of his desire to become a Louisiana legislator. He clearly was using the school board position as a stepping-stone to a higher office. But true to his message, Branch continued to cater to the District 11 voters, as did former Ku Klux Klansman David Duke, who garnered 57 percent of the vote in that district in the 1990 U.S. Senate race. If the voters in District 11 had had their way, David Duke would have been Louisiana's U.S. senator instead of J. Bennett Johnston. Branch knew that he could continue to ride that wave to the Louisiana Senate, which he did in the October 21, 1994, contest against white candidate Mike Cross in District 13.

Before his election to the Senate, Branch resigned from the board. Board members appointed Jay Devall in July 1994 to complete the three-and-a-half years left on his term. Devall was a welcome replacement for Branch because he preached a message of board unity during his campaign to fill the vacant seat. His appointment made my job of presiding at board meetings much more manageable.

A few years after leaving the school board, Branch contacted me and asked me to write a recommendation for him to attend a helicopter pilot training program. At first, it stunned me that he would make such a request following his belligerent behavior. I agreed to recommend him and did so. In my mind, his request legitimized his genuine respect for me as an individual and as a board member. He was accepted into the pilot training program, and as far as I know, he completed it successfully.

In 1983, President Ronald Reagan signed into law the federal holiday honoring Martin Luther King. King's birthday is January 15, and the federal holiday is observed on the third Monday in January of each year. Though efforts to establish the holiday began shortly after King's assassination in 1968, the holiday was not observed nationwide until 1986 and it was not celebrated in all fifty states until 2000. The failure of Congress to pass the legislation before 1983 was due to racial and political opposition. Like many other states, Louisiana did not rush to make King's birthday a state government holiday.

The Louisiana legislature approved the holiday in 2004, and Governor Kathleen Blanco signed it into law in January of 2005. The East Baton Rouge Parish School Board had begun serious discussions about declaring a holiday honoring King sometime in 1985 but did not approve it until 1987. Black citizens of East Baton Rouge Parish wanted it and fought for an official observance of the holiday. School board members opposed to the holiday espoused some of the same rhetoric used at the federal level, especially by North Carolina senators Jesse Helms and John Porter East.

Some board members felt not only that a holiday would be too expensive, but also that honoring a private citizen would be contrary to long-standing tradition, since King had never held public office. Some felt the January date was too early in the second semester to have a holiday. Others alleged that King was associated with suspected communists. Still others believed there was no connection between the holiday and the education of our children. How very wrong these ideas were. They showed then, and still show, the mindset of some of white America.

I have a good recollection of some of the discussions about declaring King's birthday a holiday, but I especially remember the decision on the type of holiday it should be. Some board members—chief among them Frank Millican Sr.—and others in the community proposed having the day off, thus allowing school administrators, faculty, staff, and students to attend community activities. I consistently argued for an in-school holiday dedicated to studying King's work and life, which would have benefited all school personnel regardless of race or ethnicity, but particularly the white students. Whites needed to learn what Black people were all about and how they lived their lives.

In Baton Rouge at least, there is still a need for that kind of education for whites. Blacks had hundreds of years to learn about whites, but white students knew little about black students. During the board's discussion of the holiday issue, I predicted that after a few years, there would be very little attendance, especially by students, at the community activities. I posited that white students were unlikely to attend celebratory activities even when the holiday was first observed. During in-school celebrations, Black and white students would have had no option but to learn about King's philosophy, life, work, and death, and the importance they had, and continue to have, to all Americans. Sadly, both of my predictions came true. I feel that the importance of King's work and existence are rapidly being lost. Many Black people, students or otherwise, don't know about him and his work or what it has meant not only to Americans but also to the whole world. The holiday honors both the individual and a struggle, which continues even today.

Millican and I often disagreed on tactics and on which aspects of issues confronting the board were most critical. However, our disagreements rarely manifested themselves in open discussions. Our disagreement about the in-school versus out-of-school King holiday was an exception. I felt very strongly about the in-school approach, and to me it was worth the open disagreement. The King holiday fight was a deep challenge for me and my school board service. I only hope that the importance of Dr. King's life will not be diminished by either the existence of the holiday or the slander of his memory by the racists in today's world.

The school board elections of 1994 ushered in a dramatic change. Nine new members were elected, and all had the backing of a business community group, Friends of CAPE, which stood for Community Action for Public Education. Members of CAPE felt that the school board needed a complete overhaul and should approach education as a business.

CAPE contended that the board, in the aftermath of years of inappropriate behavior, needed change. A local pollster, Bernie Pinsonat, opined that school board members "shot themselves so many times in the foot, it became terminal. It's a lesson in how not to get re-elected." Most incumbents chose not to seek re-election. According to CAPE, the desire for change was greatest in predominantly white districts. Voters re-elected Black incumbent Jacqueline Mims and me because sentiment for change in our districts was not as high as concern about crime.

The CAPE success story began in December 1993, when white businessman Jensen Holliday and Black minister Rev. Charles T. Smith assembled an ad-hoc steering committee with former PTA president Bernadette Wilkinson, then-current PTA president Janet Parrish, and executive director of the Istrouma Area Council of the Boys Scouts of America John Erickson.

According to CAPE co-chairman Holliday, the group's intentions were to bring together a community-wide coalition to change the philosophy of school board governance. Were these efforts designed to take over the board? Were they efforts of the Chamber of Commerce's Political Action Committee? The answer to both questions was perhaps yes; but were they necessary and beneficial to the school system? In the end, the performance of the "CAPE board" changed the discontent and cynicism of the public to such an extent that we were finally able to pass new taxes and resolve the long-standing desegregation case.

Jacqueline Mims, Mike Branch, and I were the three returning board members, and none of us were backed by CAPE. CAPE allegedly stayed out of my race for re-election, according to a December 30, 1994, story by the *Baton Rouge Advocate* news staff. A November 10 article by Mike Dunne noted that the three of us were spurned by the organization. Mims and I did gain the support of the East Baton Rouge Parish Teacher and School Employees groups. Whether CAPE supported me or not, I won re-election without a runoff. First Circuit Court of Appeal Judge Freddie Pitcher Jr., who is Black, swore me in.

The new members were Ingrid Kelley, Warren Pratt, the Reverend Leo Cyrus, Patricia Haynes Smith, Noel Hammatt, Roger Moser, Dan Henderson, Eldon Ledoux, and "Buckskin" Bill Black. I was surprised when board members indicated they wanted me to serve as their president for the 1995–96 two-year term—my second time as president—since CAPE had not endorsed me (or any incumbents, because that went against its stated goal of change). I expected individuals from among the nine new members to be selected as president and vice president, especially since the votes were there to do so. In 1997, the board broke with tradition and selected me as president for a second consecutive two-year term, making it my third time holding that office.

The 1995–98 school board was perhaps the best board the system had known in quite some time. After the election, those business-connected members soon realized that many factors had to be considered when operating a school system. I suspect that my being asked to assume the presidency was a result of that realization.

With CAPE's support, the members decided to hold a retreat to build camaraderie among themselves and to provide a learning opportunity. Following the closed-door meeting, I remarked to the news media, "I think we learned we can trust each other." Incumbent Jackie Mims said, "The retreat helped dispel some of the stereotypes we may have had about each other." Newly elected member Eldon Ledoux said he felt "the retreat was worthwhile." The group received criticism for holding a retreat that the media could not attend, but many members defended their decision to keep the press out of the workshop. New member Dan Henderson remarked, "We wanted it to ourselves," while Mims added that closing the workshop to the public allowed members to talk to each other without "all the lights and cameras." Those statements did not stop the media from expressing its disappointment about what it dubbed "a closed, secret gathering."

That was an incorrect characterization of our retreat. We were not yet a "board," since new members were not officially installed until January 1, 1995, and we therefore were free to do as we wanted. At the end of our meeting, the others requested that I represent the group before the media, alerting me to the possibility that I might be selected as the president of the board for 1995–96.

Some community citizens, including Donald J. Gogreve and William P. Rabon, came to the board members' defense and said that they were "unfairly attacked" by the media. According to the press, "The new School Board needs all the trust it can build to overcome the lack of trust generated by past boards."

Roughly fourteen years after Judge Parker had ordered the 1981 desegregation plan, only minimal dialogue had occurred between the school system and the plaintiffs. Much animosity had developed over those years, and the desegregation process was in turmoil. When I was elected president of the school board in 1995, one of my goals was to initiate discussions between the board and the plaintiffs, a task many thought impossible. Several of the newly elected board members were among the doubters, as were some members of the NAACP.

On December 27, 1995, we had our first face-to-face meeting; it lasted four-and-a-half hours. It was considered productive and resulted in a commitment to continue talking. The school system was designing a school improvement plan to go to Judge Parker. It changed much of the 1981 court order, which had resulted in widespread busing and public anger. A significant part of the proposed changes involved commitments to equalize resources among schools, including everything from basic teaching supplies to the caliber of staff, and to improve educational programs at all schools.

CHALLENGES, CHALLENGES, CHALLENGES

I hoped we were finally getting down to what I had recommended to the plaintiffs back in 1970.

NAACP president Alvin Washington argued that if all schools had the same resources and quality programs, the community would not be as concerned about busing. I felt that the community would not take our word. We had to implement the plans successfully and prove that the school board would honor its commitment to equity. The system talked about equity, yet never implemented a plan to achieve it.

It seemed to me and to other members that it would be impossible to build trust with the public if there was no trust between members of the board. I believed that our board served with dignity, proving that the retreat at least partially achieved its goal of establishing trust between its members. Yet neither the retreat, the needs of students and school personnel, nor what was best for the community was important enough to force the board to understand that "success in politics rests on the arts of communications and compromise."

In May 2002, once I was appointed chancellor of Southern University in New Orleans, I felt that my ability to serve the people of School Board District 3 had reached a serious conflict of interest. The thought had already occurred to me that perhaps I had been a school board member long enough. The time was right for new ideas, and I decided not to seek re-election. The SUNO appointment ultimately resulted in the ending of my school board service. I respectfully resigned from the school board effective August 31, 2002.

CHAPTER 9

Southern Administrative Career

Joining the Southern University administration brought some surprises. Along with most of my faculty colleagues, I had long held the idea that administrators got the big bucks but didn't do much to earn them. It didn't take me long to realize how wrong we were. I first joined the administration in August 1991 as the associate vice chancellor for academic affairs, serving in that position until December 1998.

My chemistry colleague, Dr. William Moore, was vice chancellor at the time, and I considered it a once-in-a-lifetime opportunity to work with him. This position, offered to me unexpectedly by Dr. Moore, put me in direct contact with deans and department chairs. More importantly, I also had direct contact with students, which allowed me the chance to impact many individuals' lives during my tenure as associate vice chancellor. It is gratifying when I meet former Southern students who tell me that I had a positive impact on their lives. In most instances, I never knew that I had done anything for them, let alone something that they felt had made their lives better.

My new position also allowed me to interact with the Southern University system president, Dr. Dolores R. Spikes (1989–1996), and other high-level officials at Southern and other state institutions, as well as with many politicians. Some of the Southern officials I remember most vividly are Marvin Allen (SUBR registrar), Willie C. Armstrong (SUBR director of admissions), Clayton Lewis (director of the Office of Public Contacts), Flandus McClinton (SUBR chief financial officer), Cynthia Tarver (SUBR financial aid director), and Tolar White (chief system financial officer).

Then as now, I believe policies are important, should be made only when necessary, and should be followed. I also strongly believe that policies should be reasonable and capable of operational practice. Even if a policy is determined to be faulty or irrelevant, it should be followed until revised or officially abandoned. Administrators, faculty, staff, and students all came to know that my office would attack issues head-on and resolve them fairly and efficiently in line with policy.

I made it a point to keep my superiors informed about actions I had taken or was contemplating taking, and I maintained records of significant decisions. SUBR chancellor Edward R. Jackson (1998–2007) once remarked that he had homework every night because of my various requests for information. I must say, however, that he always responded to my missives in a timely fashion.

When Dr. Moore left his position as vice chancellor for academic affairs, I served as interim vice chancellor from February to July 1998. A group of deans submitted my name to Chancellor Edward Jackson as a candidate for vice chancellor, but they also indicated I was not campaigning for the position. As a result, it was easy for me to revert to the associate's role once Chancellor Jackson selected Dr. Brenda Birkett as vice chancellor. In my conversations with Dr. Jackson about the job, he made it clear that he wanted a woman as the head of that office. I would say that he and I had a satisfactory meeting of minds as to his desires. I had the pleasure of continuing as an associate under the leadership of Dr. Birkett until December 1998.

One of my many responsibilities as associate vice chancellor was serving as chair of the Tenure and Promotions Committee. The tenure and promotion policy required that an application originate in the candidate's department, then go to the college dean, from there to the vice chancellor for academic affairs, and finally to the Tenure and Promotions Committee, which determined eligibility. The committee's recommendations went to the chief academic officer, who forwarded his/her advice to the president, who made recommendations to the Board of Supervisors. The Board of Supervisors gave final approval. I was primarily enforcing and developing policies and procedures related to academic administration, faculty, and students.

Perhaps the worst day of my Southern University administrative life occurred when I had worked as associate vice chancellor for less than a week. The vice chancellor of academic affairs tasked me with informing the Department of Biology that its current chair would be removed effectively that day and would be replaced by a member of the faculty. I had no briefing about why that move occurred or how a replacement would be selected. When the biology faculty questioned me about why the change was happening and who would be the designated replacement, I could tell them only that "I have been directed to bring you this information today, and any questions you have must be directed to the vice chancellor. I have not been provided with any explanation for this action."

In short, the meeting was contentious, and I was alone facing twelve to fifteen hostile people, some of whom strongly disagreed with the actions taken by the vice chancellor. What's more, I had no background information about the issues. After about an hour and a half of heated rhetoric, I ended the meeting by apologizing for having to deliver such a message on such short notice and for not being well versed in the issues involved.

I genuinely believe that my honesty about my lack of knowledge concerning the situation, my regret about having to deliver the shocking news, and my unhappiness about the directive to convene the meeting established a solid working foundation with the biology faculty and the academic community at Southern. As distasteful as the experience was, I never complained to the vice chancellor or other administrator about the untenable position that his directive put me in.

I must admit that I was surprised when, in 1998, Dr. Leon R. Tarver, president of the Southern system (1997–2005), requested that I move to his office as vice president of academic and student affairs. This was a surprise for two main reasons: I knew the serving VP, Dr. Lawrence Couvillion, and thought he was doing a good job; meanwhile, I was hard at work on several areas of concern in my own unit. I later learned that Couvillon was stepping down voluntarily, but the unresolved concerns in Academic Affairs remained. After much consideration, I agreed to assume the role of vice president for academic and student affairs and served in that role from November 1998 to May 2002.

Fellow members of the president's staff with whom I interacted on an ongoing basis included Tolar White, Frances Smith, Preston DeJean, Ralph Slaughter, Robyn Merrick, and Diane Craig. Top administrators under whom I worked throughout my tenure at Southern University included Presidents Dr. Felton G. Clark (1963–1968; he began his presidency in 1938), Dr. G. Leon Netterville (1968–1974), Dr. Jesse Stone (1974–1985), Dr. Joffre T. Whisenton (1985–1988), Dr. Dolores R. Spikes (1988–1997), and Dr. Leon Tarver II (1997–2005). Dr. Edward R. Jackson served as interim system president in 2005. Chancellors under whom I served were Dr. Roosevelt Steptoe (1977–1982), Dr. James J. Prestage (1982–1985), Dr. Wesley Cornelious McClure (1985–1988), Dr. Dolores R. Spikes (Interim 1988–1991), Dr. Marvin Yates (1991–1998), and Dr. Edward R. Jackson (1998–2007).

The Southern University system played an integral part in the initial development of Baton Rouge Community College (BRCC). BRCC resulted from a mandate in the 1994 desegregation settlement agreement between Louisiana and the U.S. Department of Justice that was intended to eliminate remnants of a dual-race postsecondary educational system. BRCC was officially established on June 28, 1995, and opened its doors on August 20, 1998. Its chancellor was Dr. Marion Bonaparte, who the Management Council had selected at its meeting on December 8, 1995. In a previous unanimous vote on October 16, 1995, the council had first offered the chancellor's job to SU alumnus O. Clayton Johnson, who declined after speaking with his family about whether to accept the post.

Chaired by SU board chairman Patrick Fontenot, the Management Council was the governing body for BRCC from the initial implementation of the desegregation agreement until 1998. The council consisted of the Boards of Supervisors from Louisiana State University and Southern University, and the two boards jointly administered the community college. As the associate vice chancellor for academic affairs at SUBR, I served as one of Southern's staff support representatives to the council while it was planning the eventual operation of the school.

One of the hypotheses that I continually put before the group was that bringing BRCC into existence would negatively affect SUBR. That proved to be the case, as SUBR's enrollment dipped significantly following BRCC's opening. Even today, SUBR still suffers from the enrollment of students at BRCC, many of whom most likely would have been students at Southern if the community college did not exist. This is not to say that establishing BRCC was bad for the state or the Baton Rouge area. It was detrimental to the enrollment of students at Southern in Baton Rouge.

The counterargument put forth to my hypothesis was that students attending BRCC (or other two-year colleges) would, upon graduation, enroll in a four-year institution, namely Southern, in sufficient numbers to offset the initial decrease in Southern's enrollment. I insisted that that premise was faulty because national statistics showed that the transfer rate from community colleges to four-year institutions was relatively low. My point became clear in the fall of 2001 when local community colleges saw a dramatic jump in enrollment while the state's public and private universities reported more modest increases or even declines in their student head counts.

The enrollment dip at SUNO was worrisomely large (about 7 percent for 2001 and 9 percent for 2002), which greatly concerned my administration. At the same time, Nunez Community College in Chalmette, which opened in 1992, reported an 18 percent jump in enrollments. Baton Rouge Community College, which opened in 1998, saw a 16 percent increase. Delgado Community College, founded in 1921 and the state's oldest and largest two-year school, recorded an 18 percent increase. Meanwhile LSU reported just a 1 percent increase in its enrollment, and Southeastern Louisiana University had a 5 percent increase. The enrollment numbers offered evidence that community colleges were becoming a force in Louisiana higher education.

To exacerbate the problem, the Board of Regents hired a Colorado-based consulting firm, Noel-Levitz, to help execute a master plan that was expected to force thousands of students into the state's community colleges beginning in 2005. The plan called for standards of admission to increase at most of the state's four-year universities in fall of 2005. That action was expected to direct thousands of first-year students with marginal academic credentials into the state's community colleges, and it did just that. The issue for the four-year schools was how to offset the loss of students—and their tuition fees—due to higher admission standards. Some schools are still recuperating.

A secondary concern was that BRCC would be the first new school in a system of community colleges scattered across the state. Lawmakers had proposed five additional community colleges, to be located in Opelousas, New Iberia, Ascension Parish, the Florida Parishes area, and the West Bank of New Orleans. There was serious concern that the other community colleges might drain funding from the court-mandated Baton Rouge school. Moreover, the state could hardly afford to repeat the largesse demanded by the proliferation of vo-tech schools back in the 1970s, when each legislator had to have at least one and got it. In April 1995, the state had forty-five vo-tech schools.

Today, BRCC is a member of the Louisiana Community and Technical College System (LCTCS). It has close to 8,200 students and eight campus sites. After twenty-six years of operation, it is the city's second-largest higher education institution. LSU is the largest, and SUBR is the third largest.

When Mike Foster became governor in 1996, his commissioner of administration, Mark Drennen, became a dominant force interacting with the Management Council of BRCC. He exhibited a tireless desire to bring the community college into existence and made the major decisions about its site location and buildings. As commissioner of administration, he had the authority and power to get whatever he wanted, including evicting the Louisiana State Police from its longtime headquarters on North Foster Drive, which is now the main campus of BRCC. Some felt that Drennen's interjecting himself into the site selection process and the timing of his involvement were serious deterrents to getting the college up and running by the consent decree date of fall 1997. Delays pushed the opening back to August 20, 1998.

Amidst this confusion, Governor Mike Foster advocated for restructuring the higher education system in the state. His ideas appeared to range from a single-board concept to one consisting of three management boards, rather than the four that existed at the time, without a Board of Regents. That debate, which began in 1996, was far above my level of influence and was adequately defended by the SU Board of Supervisors and System President Dolores Spikes. The three-board concept consisted of one board to govern LSU, the LSU Law Center, the LSU Agricultural Center, and the LSU Medical Center; a second board to govern Southern University's Baton Rouge campus, its law center, and its agricultural center; and a third board to govern all other state universities, including the state's regional universities and Grambling State University, an HBCU. This third board would thus also oversee Southern University's New Orleans and Shreveport campuses, as well as the other schools in the LSU system: the University of New Orleans, LSU Shreveport, LSU Alexandria, and LSU Eunice.

Southern University and its supporters opposed Governor Foster's restructuring plan out of concern that the Southern University system would be demolished. The current Board of Regents and four management boards finally resulted.

CHAPTER 10

Other System Positions

Serving the Southern University system as vice president was exciting, especially because I was often asked to represent President Leon Tarver at private and public meetings and events. This enabled me to meet some truly remarkable people, such as Nelson Mandela and Steve Harvey. But even more interesting were my tenures as interim chancellor at Southern University New Orleans (SUNO) and at Southern University Shreveport-Bossier (SUSBO). Each of these interim assignments was to fill in as the chancellor while the system searched to find a permanent one. In those circumstances, I never relinquished my position as vice president until my second stint at SUNO.

My first interim assignment was at SUNO in March of 2000. President Tarver led a focused search for a new chancellor, assisted by a committee representing all major constituents of SUNO and the Southern system. As a member of the search committee, I spent a sizable portion of my monthlong stint on that effort. The candidate favored by the faculty, Dr. Joseph Bouie, received the committee's approval to shepherd the four-year campus going forward. Dr. Bouie was a longtime SUNO faculty member, and his desire to be chancellor was well known.

My second interim assignment was at the Shreveport-Bossier campus in the fall of 2000. Immediately, I was confronted with the issue of the school's name. The Louisiana Board of Regents had informed the campus and system that "Bossier" was not officially a part of the school's name and had to be removed. We could no longer refer to the school as Southern University Shreveport-Bossier. I immediately requested suggestions for new names, which would be reviewed by the chancellor's office and discussed with various university constituents in order to come to a final decision.

At the conclusion of that process, I recommended to President Tarver that the new name be Southern University at Shreveport, Louisiana, abbreviated SUSLA. He agreed and submitted the proposed name to the system's Board of Supervisors, who approved it. But the process was somewhat contentious at first, because many people believed that Bossier was an official part of the name and had been using it to represent the campus since its inception. (The school had opened for instruction during the administration of Governor John McKeithen, on September 19, 1967.) But the selected name, SUSLA, was well received by the university community and, as far as I know, by the Board of Regents.

Another contentious issue at SUSLA involved the policy of renting a portion of its downtown campus for outside activities. Almost as soon as I arrived on campus, I learned that the director used her discretion to determine the rental fees charged. As might be expected, this generated a host of complaints. I charged the director to develop policies that could be applied consistently by any employee who was given the authorization to lease the premises. She viewed this request as diminishing her authority, and she involved a system board member in the ensuing conflict.

After meeting with various parties and assuring them that I was not seeking to dismiss the employee but simply to set up viable working policies, the atmosphere changed. New policies were developed and implemented, and they worked wonderfully. It's surprising how little things can get blown out of proportion and interfere with orderly operations, particularly when superiors inject themselves into situations. It helped tremendously that I had the support and counsel of my vice chancellor for student affairs, Dr. Ray L. Belton, current Southern system president and a longtime employee at SUSLA. (The system president is also the chancellor of the Baton Rouge campus.) Our working relationship was such that he was a constant source of collaboration about issues at the school. I remember Dr. Belton being somewhat hesitant to apply for the chancellorship of

SUSLA because he feared he wasn't qualified for the position. I told him I was sure he had what it took and strongly urged him to apply. When I ended my interim stint as chancellor at SUSLA, the Board of Supervisors named him as the new chancellor of the two-year campus.

My third interim chancellor's job was again at Southern University at New Orleans, in February–May 2002. When I was approached about the position, the teacher education programs at both SUNO and SUBR were under attack. SUNO had narrowly dodged a contentious effort to suspend its teacher training program at an August 2001 meeting of the Board of Elementary and Secondary Education (BESE). I addressed BESE in my capacity as system vice president for academic and student affairs and said I was confident that students at the Baton Rouge and New Orleans campuses were getting better training and that PRAXIS passage rates would improve. BESE voted to keep its 2001 decision to give the New Orleans campus until the end of the spring 2003 semester to solve the problems in its teacher-training program and earn national accreditation or lose its state approval. It was a difficult task but not impossible, and it was achieved. At the time, SUBR and other teacher-prep programs were also about to face intense scrutiny under Louisiana's effort at improving teacher training.

To make matters worse, the Board of Supervisors had fired SUNO chancellor Joseph Bouie on January 11, 2002. Board members cited a damaging audit that harshly criticized Bouie's fiscal management. Bouie claimed that the real reason for his ouster was that he had fired the wife of U.S. Representative William Jefferson from her post as vice chancellor for academic affairs. I had no part in the Andrea Jefferson matter except to advise Bouie off the record not to proceed with her removal. The resulting dispute about the firings was hot and fueled speculation about a political conspiracy theory. Rumors swirled, and positions for or against the firings hardened.

Thus, when President Tarver approached me about assuming the interim chancellorship of SUNO, at first I said that I did not want to accept the position. Having observed the Gerald Peoples and Joseph Bouie firings, being aware of the problems with BESE, knowing about the toxic political atmosphere in New Orleans and at SUNO, remembering the utter disdain of the Faculty Senate for previous administrations, taking into account the adverse audit by legislative auditor Dan Kyle, being aware of the ongoing management issues at SUNO, and having serious concerns about the financial health of the school, I had no appetite to lead the SUNO campus. I told President Tarver that I felt that taking the interim chancellor's job at SUNO would end my career in the Southern University system. He assured me that would not be the case.

Critical to my consenting to be interim chancellor was an agreement that I be allowed to take a financial expert with me to help put the financial side of the university in tip-top shape and in whom I could place my trust. With that request approved by President Tarver, I selected the Southern University system's top internal auditor, Gloria Thompson, as interim vice chancellor for administration. The Board of Supervisors later approved my choice.

Shortly after our arrival, on February 10, 2002, I learned that the school was in danger of losing its College of Education and its teacher training program. The potential losses were due to action by the Louisiana Board of Regents, the agency created by the 1974 state constitution as the coordinator of public higher education in the state. My understanding, which proved to be accurate, was that there was no time to seek another chancellor, and I requested that President Tarver elevate me from interim chancellor to chancellor.

My appointment became official on May 11, 2002. With it, I inherited the long-term leadership of a four-year institution of higher education that had in place only one out of three vice chancellors, no deans, one or two department chairs, and a myriad of well-known financial issues. One of those vacant dean positions was for the College of Education, which also lacked an associate dean.

Furthermore, the College of Education had failed to attain accreditation by the National Council for Accreditation of Teacher Education (NCATE) for more than twelve years. In May 2002, NCATE visited the college and determined that it could not evaluate the school's programs because of the lack of stable leadership at both the university and college levels. The accreditation team gave "extreme instability" at SUNO and in its College of Education as the reason for its decision. The team terminated its on-site visit and vowed not to return anytime soon. The Board of Regents thus directed that the college cease accepting students in the education program by the end of the 2003 spring semester. I knew that there was no way to get NCATE back to review our programs without putting in place the administrative leadership hierarchy the university lacked. Our course of action was clear.

By the time of the Bayou Classic on November 30, 2002, I had hired Dr. Rose Duhon Sells, former dean of the College of Education at SUBR, as SUNO's dean; she reluctantly came out of retirement at my insistence. Accreditation preparations were completed, NCATE returned and carried through its review, and the College of Education was accredited. What's more, we were well on our way to filling the various interim positions with permanent appointees.

It was a particular highlight for me when I convinced the retired Dr. E. C. Harrison to take on the job of vice chancellor for academic affairs at SUNO following the resignation of my first appointee, Dr. Henry Hardy. I was pleased with Hardy's development as vice chancellor, and his sudden resignation without explanation is still a mystery. However, I firmly believe that his resignation resulted from pressure from certain Faculty Senate members who wanted our administration to fail. Dr. Harrison had served as dean and vice president for academic affairs at SUBR, as well as vice president, dean of the university, and dean of the Graduate School at Dillard University. What a twist of fate . . . Dr. Harrison had hired me as an assistant professor of chemistry at SUBR back in 1963. Forty years later, I hired him as my vice chancellor for academic affairs.

I believe that I was a strong campus advocate without having to challenge system executives. We were an essential part of the Southern University system and an essential part of the system team. For the most part, I was left to govern the campus as I thought best. My roadmap to restoring calm consisted of being fair to administrators, faculty, staff, and students; being consistent and focused on the betterment of the school; constructing a team comprised of people who were committed to doing what was correct and helpful to the school; having an open-door policy; and curing the school's financial ills. I considered Joe Bouie—who remained at the university as a faculty member in the School of Social Work—a friend, just as he had been before losing the chancellorship. I made it a point to offer a handshake, embrace, smile, and so forth whenever I had the opportunity. I did not dwell on things that happened in his past.

I felt very prepared to serve as chancellor and attribute much of my confidence to the Nissan-ETS Fellows Program I participated in during 2000 and 2001. The Nissan Motor Corporation sponsored the program in partnership with the Educational Testing Service. It was designed to expose potential Black leaders from HBCUs to various aspects of leadership in an institution of higher education. The program concentrated on such topics as leadership style, financial principles, academic prowess, political savvy, and administrative integrity. The number of participants who later became leaders of HBCUs or other institutions of higher learning testifies to the quality of the program. Concepts and techniques I learned in the program supplemented those I had acquired through the Southern University system and MEL, Inc.

My biggest disappointment while serving as chancellor was my inability to establish a working relationship with the SUNO Faculty Senate, even though I tried. I invited Dr. William Stewart, president of the Senate, to sit down with me to discuss a wide range of topics, including budgets, faculty and staff appointments, and promotions. I explained in detail the choices facing the administration, as well as why we did what we did. He indicated that he fully understood and agreed that the actions taken were necessary and above board.

After leaving the meeting, however, Dr. Stewart criticized the administration for its actions and accused it of violating policies and procedures. It became clear that the Senate's intent was not to improve SUNO but to antagonize the administration. Unfortunately, life does not always unfold as one wishes it to. But some hidden gems often took the sting away when life did not go as expected. For example, when I took over as chancellor of SUNO, our slogan was "Putting Academics First." By December 2002, for the first time in many years, the university made headlines for its programs rather than for political infighting. Some of the more pleasurable developments during my SUNO chancellorship were my interactions with the students and faculty of the School of Music and the Department of Biology, as well as the formation of the Museum Studies Program.

Edward "Kidd" Jordan, associate professor of music at SUNO, was also a professional musician who played musical dates throughout the United States, Europe, and Asia as his schedule allowed. He prided himself on being a practical teacher. Jordan saw New Orleans and south Louisiana as places having an incredible wealth of raw musical talent. Many gifted young performers came to SUNO with stars in their eyes, some going on to become full-time, professional musicians who traveled the world playing New Orleans jazz or rock 'n' roll.

Jordan's advice to most was that they could make an excellent living as music teachers while playing professionally on the side to the extent that they wished. While New Orleans area musicians were keenly aware of SUNO's School of Music and the expertise of Kidd Jordan and his colleagues, most of the public was not. I hoped to help the program grow to double or triple its 2002 size while offering a bachelor's degree and workshops for outstanding students at the college, high school, and elementary school levels, while at the same time still sending those musical ambassadors worldwide.

Another hidden SUNO gem was Dr. David Adegboye, chair of the biology department. Adegboye, a doctoral graduate of Cambridge University, was working with determination to build up a strong department. It was working; the department had been sending a steady stream of graduates to pharmacy, medical, and health schools since he had arrived at SUNO. He introduced molecular biology and pathogenic microbiology/immunology to the department's curriculum. Statewide, only about half of Louisiana's universities and colleges offered molecular biology.

Dr. Adegboye personified the SUNO faculty's excellence, which for many years took a back seat to the political chaos that often rocked the campus. The fact that 80 percent of SUNO's student body held full-time jobs while going to school and, in many cases, supporting families also led to the widely held belief that SUNO's students were marginal students. Both Adegboye and I begged to differ.

Adegboye said, "It takes a very special, dedicated kind of student to leap into a demanding science curriculum while holding a full-time job and family responsibilities. But neither the full-time job nor the family responsibilities negate the quality of the student's mind or their burning desire to succeed and achieve their dreams. If anything, the drive and ambition of our science students increase the pressure on our faculty to nurture, encourage, and assist our students in realizing their hopes. That's our challenge." Dr. Adegboye is still sending students to schools in the health fields.

Another joy during my tenure as chancellor was establishing a master of arts in the museum studies program at SUNO. The school owned an extensive collection of African art, but it struggled to maintain and preserve the collection and largely kept it hidden. Before I arrived in 2002, some people had thought about forming a museum studies program that could assist with use and maintenance of the collection. Statistics revealed that in the New Orleans area, a museum mecca with nearly fifty museums, there were few minorities active in museum-related work. That was true in New Orleans, and it was also evident throughout the United States.

Convinced of the need to develop more equitable, diverse, and inclusive cultural institutions, I wholeheartedly endorsed the concept of a Master of Arts in Museum Studies Program (MAMSP). Its mission would be to educate and train a diverse student population through a balanced approach between theory and practice, and to graduate professionals and leaders in the museum and arts sectors. As the only such program in Louisiana, SUNO's MAMSP would position itself as a significant regional and national hub for intellectual discussions in the museum studies discipline, particularly around diversity, inclusion, and social justice issues in museums.

This unique program would further SUNO's "Academics First" philosophy, grow its student population and the university, contribute significantly to a void in the cultural environment of our country, and at the same time, further signal that SUNO was a legitimate higher education institution. We were fortunate to hire Redell Hearn as the graduate program director to bring about this transformation. Ms. Hearn was well-trained, knowledgeable, and had excellent connections to the museum world in New Orleans and beyond.

OTHER SYSTEM POSITIONS

Once the program was established, SUNO began to teach students the theories, procedures, and managerial concepts of museums. SUNO's program would eventually find itself in dialogue with various local, regional, and national museums, campus museums, private galleries, and historical associations.

In early January 2005, I attended an evaluation session with President Tarver before participating in a Board of Supervisors meeting on the Baton Rouge campus. I had wondered why my evaluation was taking so long, since I knew that other chancellors' reviews had been completed some time ago. During my meeting with President Tarver, I learned the reason for the delay: I supposedly did not have a good handle on the finances at SUNO. Yet the campus was in the best financial shape it had seen in many years. My team and I had completed several critical program enhancements, corrected the instability of the administrative team, and increased enrollment and fundraising. Having observed the terminations of Dr. Gerald Peoples and Dr. Joseph Bouie, I immediately realized that a justification was underway to relieve me of my post, which had nothing to do with any problem at the school. Quite frankly, I had not yet considered leaving my post as chancellor. But with my realization that an excuse was being fabricated to fire me, I refused to participate in that process and informed President Tarver that I would retire before allowing SUNO and myself to be the subject of such treatment. I left that meeting and shortly thereafter joined the SU Board of Supervisors meeting. At the end of my chancellor's report, I announced that I was retiring effective June 30, 2005.

My announcement came as a complete surprise to my administrative staff, and I apologized to them for dropping a bombshell. Under normal circumstances, I would have discussed such action with them beforehand. I would have preferred to have informed the faculty, other staff, and students before making my announcement. I never thought that finding my replacement would fall to me, but it did. I tip my hat to Dr. Robert Gex for accepting my invitation to assume the interim chancellor's position and thank the Board of Supervisors for taking my recommendation.

* * *

My administration at SUNO was proud of its accomplishments. We improved the image of the school in the community, state and nation; achieved NCATE accreditation of the College of Education; revised the student financial aid policies to prevent Department of Education penalties; strengthened financial and administrative policies, procedures, and actions; increased enrollment; stabilized the organizational structure; and repaid $1.05 million in Pell grants and other federal aid that had been awarded to unqualified students during the 2000–2001 school year, a debt our administration had no part in accumulating.

A direct sign of SUNO's improved community image was our ability to raise, for the first time, serious monies for the school through the establishment and implementation of the "BASH" fundraiser in 2004. The BASH, named in honor of longtime SUNO chancellor Emmett Bashful, raised more than $1,925,000 in 2004 and 2005. (Previously, the most significant annual fundraising amount was close to $22,000.) In two years, we had raised most of the required funds to set up two Eminent Scholars Endowed Chairs—the Bashful Chair in Leadership and Public Policy (BASH I) and the Millie Charles Chair in Social Work (BASH II)—which required investments of $1 million each. We operated under a revised Board of Regents policy, which reversed the usual fundraising formula of $600,000 raised and $400,000 from the Endowed Chairs fund. The set-up of the Millie Charles Chair was delayed as the BASH II came up about $75,000 short due to Hurricane Katrina, but it eventually did happen. The BASH is still active today.

Why is the image of a school important? Image affects faculty, staff, and student recruiting; fundraising; interactions and cooperative endeavors with other institutions and entities; and faculty, staff, and student morale. SUNO's new image had as its basis the three strategic plan goals of Increased Opportunities for Student Access and Success; Ensuring Quality and Accountability; and Enhancing Service to the Community and State.

Long before I arrived in 2002, SUNO was too often referred to as a glorified high school. I was determined to convert those negative inferences into positive ones concerning a bona fide institution of higher education. To bring my intent to fruition, I began actively involving myself in a series of education and civic-related organizations in the metropolitan New Orleans area. I joined the New Orleans Chamber of Commerce; the Rotary Club of New Orleans; the FBI Citizens Academy and Academy Alumni; the Executive Board of the Institute for Education and Research; the Federal Executive Board; the Greater New Orleans Education Foundation; the World Trade Center Board of Directors; the Southeast Louisiana Council of Boy Scouts of America; and the Louisiana Resource Center for Educators Board.

My active membership in such groups made it possible for me to meet and interact with many of New Orleans's top citizens, as well as education and business leaders. In those settings, I emphasized the efforts being made to upgrade SUNO's educational standards, stabilize administrative personnel and policies, set up solid financial policies and procedures, raise funds, and effectively recruit students. After a year spent implementing and spreading the word about these improvements, the image of SUNO as a glorified high school was no longer prevalent. By the time my administration ended, SUNO was in a tremendous fundraising mode, enrollment was growing steadily, the administration was stable, and finances were in perhaps their best shape in a long time. Two of the most effective image builders for the university were the Chancellor's TV Show and the revised SUNO Journal.

Another positive image builder for SUNO was my involvement with the residents of Pontchartrain Park, a community close to the SUNO campus that was seeking a spot on the National Register of Historic Places. Developed in the early or mid-1950s, Pontchartrain Park was New Orleans's first middle- and upper-middle-class Black subdivision. SUNO's African and African-American Studies Center served as the repository for memorabilia from the community that was to be forwarded to the National Register.

A number of civic, business, political, and educational leaders formed the Pontchartrain Park Project Committee to ensure that "the Park" got the historical recognition it deserved. Committee membership included me as SUNO's chancellor. In SUNO's early days, many faculty members lived in Pontchartrain Park; many still do today. The final document collection ended at SUNO on November 21, 2003, but we received no notice of acceptance or rejection to the National Register prior to my retirement.

May 8, 2004, was a historic day for SUNO. The school hosted Senator John Kerry, the Democratic nominee for president of the United States. It was graduation day for SUNO, and having Senator Kerry visit the campus and speak to our graduates was a treat. The university had originally asked defense attorney Johnnie Cochran Jr. to be the commencement speaker. Following initial contact with Cochran's scheduler, I spoke with Attorney Cochran several times, and then with Mrs. Cochran on two or three occasions, which was a pleasure. It turned out that Johnnie had an undisclosed neurological condition. Mrs. Cochran was very pleasant and kept me generally informed about Johnnie's condition, but it became obvious after my third conversation with her that Johnnie was not going to keep his commitment to us. At that point, graduation day was not far off, and my planners and I were in a mad scramble to find a replacement speaker.

With the help of U.S. Representative William Jefferson, Senator Kerry became our "Man on Point." We soon learned, however, that having Senator Kerry as the commencement speaker was not necessarily the best thing to do. The publicity was great, but the security headache was a nightmare. The senator's security people literally took over our arrangements, telling us what we could and could not do. Thereafter it was decided we would never again ask such a high-profile individual to be our commencement speaker.

Statewide, I served as chair of the executive committee of the Louisiana Campus Compact (LACC), which consisted of twenty-six of Louisiana's thirty higher education institutions. The state was the 31st to form a group affiliated with the Campus Compact organization, which was based at Brown University. Strongly supported by Commissioner of Higher Education Joseph Savoie and approved by the Louisiana Board of Regents, the Compact existed to share information about programs staffed by college students who, among other things, tutored public school students, designed parks, assisted the elderly, and planted trees—in short, students who were involved in service learning. We were unsuccessful in convincing LSU, the state's flagship university, to join us in the LACC cooperative.

OTHER SYSTEM POSITIONS

My closest associate in the New Orleans education community was Dr. Norman C. Francis, president of Xavier University of Louisiana. We often attended the same national meetings and conferred about common institutional interests; sometimes we socialized together. Seeing Dr. Francis at meetings was exhilarating because usually I would be the only Black face in the audience. I regularly joked with Dr. Francis about his longevity as Xavier's leader (1968–2015) and asked him about when he would retire. His response was always "one of these days."

Dr. Francis was a brilliant scholar and tenacious fundraiser who was well liked and admired by many. It was an absolute joy to converse with him. When he did retire in 2015, I knew that he gave his all to his beloved Xavier University of Louisiana. Hats off to a great leader from Lafayette, Louisiana, and a Presidential Medal of Freedom awardee.

When I left the SUNO chancellorship, Entergy New Orleans was considering donating a portion of its old power station building at 1600 Peters Street to SUNO. It was to be renovated for commercial use with a dedicated space for SUNO, and it would provide a long-term source of income for the university. This was intended to be a cooperative effort between the Slave Ship Museum, Entergy New Orleans, and SUNO.

Dan Packer, Entergy's president, was the central mover behind this effort, but he became ill and retired. I have no information about the present status of the Peters Street Project, but I supported it 100 percent. SUNO's participation in that cooperative venture had the potential to build a financial foundation for the school the likes of which it had never known before.

I announced to the Board of Supervisors on January 8, 2005, that I would retire from SUNO and the system on June 30. During the six-month period between the announcement of my retirement and its effective date, I reflected often upon my prediction to Dr. Tarver—which turned out to be correct—that accepting the leadership role at SUNO would end my career in the Southern University system. What I did not anticipate was that Dr. Tarver's system presidency would end also on June 30, 2005.

On June 17, 2005, the system sponsored an event celebrating our joint retirements at the upscale Plimsoll Club, located in the World Trade Center in New Orleans. I must pay homage to many of the system's administrators, faculty, and staff for their support of our administrative efforts over the years. A final demonstration of this support and appreciation for our work was on display at this event, which was very well designed and attended. In addition to SUNO personnel and friends, the crowd included representatives from the Southern University system; the New Orleans City Council; the Office of the Mayor; and members of the Louisiana legislature, the Alpha Phi Alpha fraternity, and Camphor Memorial United Methodist Church. I extend many thanks to all who came to the event, and to those who presented certificates, plaques, and other memorabilia. It was especially pleasing to have my friend Fred Bell present and able to share those moments with me.

Until the final day of my SUNO leadership, efforts to expand and strengthen the school were at the forefront of everything we did. I harbor no ill will toward the university system with regard to my departure: *to everything there is a season, and a time to every purpose under heaven.* I am proud that I spent my entire career attending or assisting HBCUs.

Incidentally and strangely, as I wrote this section of my book on August 30, 2021, a category 4 hurricane named Ida (sporting sustained winds of 150 mph at coastal landing) had just passed through Greater Baton Rouge and southeastern Louisiana, leaving 1.1 million homes and businesses without electrical power (out of only about 2 million utility customers in the entire state). It was sixteen years to the day since Hurricane Katrina devastated New Orleans and other parts of southeastern Louisiana.

Damages from Katrina were extensive, as was the devastation following Ida. Both hurricanes were major in scope, size, and effects, but Katrina affected my family and me more than Ida did. When Katrina came ashore in August 2005, I was in the process of moving our family back to our Baton Rouge home. With an apartment lease expiring on August 31, I was content to slowly bring our possessions from New Orleans back to Baton Rouge. My wife, Ruth, was more eager to do so, however, and she told me on Saturday, August 22, that she was tired of us dilly-dallying around with our belongings. She felt we should pack everything into the car "NOW."

OTHER SYSTEM POSITIONS

We did just that, returned to Baton Rouge, and never got a chance to go back to our apartment on West End Boulevard in Metairie. After the storm passed, we learned that the apartment building sustained twelve feet of floodwater. Someone in heaven above was indeed looking out for us that day and the following days. We were finally able to close the lease sometime in 2007.

I vividly remember my conversations with New Orleanians about whether they would evacuate the city as Katrina approached. Every person I spoke with said that they had weathered hurricanes before and would ride this one out as well. No one foresaw the possibility of such devastation as Katrina wreaked. Still, I thought it would be safer to be in Baton Rouge than to stay below sea level in New Orleans. God smiled on my family as we wrestled with the decision we had to make.

CHAPTER 11

Life after Southern

During my 42-year career in the Southern University system, I rarely attended any of the excellent sporting events in which the university participated. I was simply too busy to do so, except on weekends. I was primarily a football fan and made it a point to attend every home game, as well as every Bayou Classic since its 1974 inception (except one in the 2000s and some away games). I was in Tulane Stadium for the first Bayou Classic, and I look forward to attending many more.

One of the advantages of retirement is that I now have time to participate in whatever sporting activities I choose. I became a season book holder for football, basketball, and baseball. Attendance at away games has now become commonplace. The Southern University Jaguars take sports seriously, and their play takes a backseat to no other program. But one cannot talk about, think about, or see football at Southern without the university band, the Human Jukebox from Jaguar Land. Considered throughout the United States to be one of the most talented, artistic, and musically adept groups, the Human Jukebox performs at a wide variety of venues.

In 2007, I received a request to lend my name to a bold effort to form an online university, Duplichain University, by principal owner Dr. Rose Duhon Sells, who I had lured out of retirement to lead the SUNO College of Education in 2002. I expected that Duplichain would use my name only for licensure by the Louisiana Board of Regents. I was happy to oblige since Dr. Sells had done such an excellent job in getting the SUNO College of Education accredited.

LIFE AFTER SOUTHERN

At its meeting on July 3, 2008, the Board of Trustees of Duplichain University officially appointed me president of the school. My tenure ended when the university failed to earn accreditation by the Southern Association of Colleges and Schools (SACS). I thus retired for the third time in January 2015.

Working with Dr. Sells and other parties on behalf of Duplichain University was very rewarding. My primary role as president was to promote the institution publicly and privately, and also to fundraise for its operations. Seeking investment funds would come later. As time went on, however, it became clear that I needed to address operational policies, procedures, day-to-day management, approvals by the Louisiana Board of Regents, and SACS accreditation. These requirements severely limited my quest for funding, and financial stability/viability were the main detriments to Duplichain's accreditation by SACS. Without SACS accreditation, the Board of Regents could not, by law, continue to approve the operations of the university. Duplichain University awarded ten master's degrees and ten doctorates in its short existence.

Oddly, I sought none of the career jobs or positions I have held. Each one came because someone made me an offer at the right time when I could accept without regrets. I enjoyed every position I ever held. For that, I consider myself blessed and am eternally grateful. I believe that by any reasonable standard, my career has been a successful one. At the very least, it has been enjoyable. I live by the adage I taught my students and shared with anyone who had an interest: "Do your best every time. When you have done that, there is no need to fret, worry about what you have done, or second-guess yourself. Once your best has been put forth, there is nothing else you can do." This attitude has spared me much heartache and regrets.

Individuals and organizations have acknowledged my life's activities, locally, regionally, and nationally. I have received numerous honors and awards from various organizations, and I have participated in several professional groups: the American Chemical Society, Sigma Xi, Phi Beta Kappa, Beta Kappa Chi, and the Louisiana Academy of Sciences. I am listed in *Who's Who among American High School Students* (1982–1983),

Who's Who in the South and Southwest (1969–1970, 1971–1972), *Personalities of the South* (1970), and *Men and Women of Science and Outstanding Young Men of America* (1972 edition). In 1978, the Legal Aid Society of Baton Rouge honored me with the Outstanding Service Award as chairman (1975–77). No matter what activities garnered my attention, I always found time to engage with the community and church activities.

Along the path of life, many things impact us. Some of those are disappointing, but others are rewarding. Small as some may be, they can have a positive effect on what we consider enjoyment. I recollect how much fun it was for me to serve as the emcee for the Miss Talented Teen Pageant, a national pageant program, in 1979 and 1980.

The pageant consisted of middle school students displaying their talents. The level of sophistication with which they performed was unbelievable, and I watched the judges struggle to determine the winners. Many times it seemed desirable to give each participant an award, but that was not possible. It was so much fun watching the winners' celebrations, but it broke my heart to see the losers' sorrow.

I always let the contestants know that each of them was a winner just because of their talent and their willingness to put it on display. Those young people would sing, dance, play an instrument, or perform a recitation, each to the delight of the audience. Once I even tried singing, "There She Is" after the announcement of the top winner as she paraded around the stage. But my singing did not go as well as I would have liked, so I never did it again.

During the Miss Plus America pageant, another national pageant program for which I served as a judge in 2005 and 2009, a different picture emerged. This three-day pageant consisted of unique and beautiful delegates who competed for the coveted title. There were Mrs., Ms., Miss, and Teen divisions. The judges' job was to determine the perfect representative in each division. That representative would be the sort of person who could be surprised with a press conference but who would not waver in giving astute answers on command. What's more, the winners would be people who were responsible with their time. Each took her platform, as well as the title, seriously and would dedicate her time to making appearances. Many of the women were frequent pageant participants.

There were strict guidelines concerning the judges' behavior while at the pageant. Basically, judges were to have no contact with the contestants, their families, or the media. Like the Talented Teen program, the Miss Plus America pageant was difficult to judge because the contestants were all so very talented, well dressed, and beautiful. In addition to observing the great talent, it was intriguing to watch the dynamics between the contestants and other elements of the pageant, such as how the contestants behaved before the judges. Again, it was a pleasure to be involved with such an activity.

My two sons have turned something I said once while emceeing a pageant into a lifelong joke. Once there were problems with the audio system, delaying the beginning of the event. I believe in being on time, and I could feel the audience getting restless. So, to calm their impatience, I walked out on stage and announced, "Sorry for the delay, folks, we are having technical difficulties." The boys thought that was the funniest thing ever, and they never let me forget it. They make joking references about my "technical difficulties" to this day.

An interesting sidebar occurred in my life in 1988, when I served as the chairman of the annual awards dinner for the local chapter of the National Conference of Christians and Jews (NCCJ), now the National Conference for Community and Justice. The dinner that year honored Carolyn Woodfin Carnahan and Josef Sternberg as winners of the organization's Brotherhood/Sisterhood Awards. I was fortunate to receive the 50th Annual Brotherhood Award on February 26, 1998. Sue Wilbert Turner received the Sisterhood Award that year.

I worked with the Baton Rouge chapter of the NCCJ for many years. The NCCJ is a nonprofit human relations organization engaged in a nationwide effort to eliminate prejudice and discrimination through education. The organization strives to build better relationships among people of all religions, races, and nationalities. At present, the Brotherhood/Sisterhood awards recognize individuals in the Greater Baton Rouge area who are advocates for humanitarian service. The awards are housed at the Capital Area United Way, their permanent host organization.

Since 2002, I've worked with several community-based organizations and church groups in Baton Rouge, some of which are not mentioned here. After retiring from a career in education, I have spent my time serving in leadership roles at Camphor Memorial United Methodist Church and the Municipal Fire and Police Civil Service Board. I am also an active member of Together Baton Rouge and Together Louisiana.

At Camphor, I served as a member and president of the United Methodist men and as chair of the higher education ministry. I am serving a ten-year stint as church lay leader, whose job it is to advocate for and represent the laity in the congregation; I also serve as the liaison between the pastor and the church membership. As an extension of the congregation in the community, the lay leader needs to be aware of the reputation the church has in the community and work to enhance it. The lay leader also advocates for the needs of the community and encourages the congregation to care for those beyond the church walls.

The Municipal Fire and Police Civil Service Board consists of five voting members and has its own legal counsel. One member is elected by the employees of the fire service from among their rank. One member is elected by the employees of the police service from among their rank. The Metro Council appoints the other three members. Board members have a responsibility to use common sense, discern given a set of circumstances, and exhibit a sense of justice and fairness.

In my early years on the board, employees of the fire and police services were reasonable in their requests regarding appeals, most of which were in the area of discipline. However, the appointment in 2018 of a Black police chief, Murphy J. Paul Jr., who professed a desire to change the way that the police department operated, resulted in a flood of requests appealing disciplinary actions he had imposed.

Such appeals sometimes required long hours of deliberations. One board meeting lasted sixteen hours straight. The issue at hand was whether the chief had acted in good faith. After several three-year terms on the board, and also serving as vice chair, I have developed a distaste for the manner in which some police officers (almost all of them white) have used the system. In the case of Chief Paul, there appeared to be a serious clash between the police chief and the white officers who resisted changes in police behavior. As of this writing, a new, white police chief has been installed in Baton Rouge. How his tenure will play out remains to be seen.

Together Baton Rouge (TBR) is a broad-based coalition of congregations and community-based organizations in the Greater Baton Rouge area. It has the capacity to address community problems both large and small. The alliance deliberately crosses the lines of race, religion, neighborhood, and political affiliation. It works on issues affecting families and communities in a strictly nonpartisan way.

TBR has three primary goals: to build relationships across our community based on trust and willingness to listen to each other; to equip our members and leadership with skills and practices to get results; and to achieve change on concrete issues as a part of our standard call to justice.

Together Louisiana (TLA) is a statewide network of more than 250 religious congregations and civic organizations across Louisiana, representing more than 200,000 people. It is one of the largest grassroots organizations in the history of Louisiana. Its mission is to allow faith and community-based organizations to develop the leadership capacity of their members and to work together to effect change on a larger scale than they could alone.

TLA is currently addressing issues of tax fairness, access to healthcare, flood recovery, access to healthy food, workforce development, criminal justice reform, redistricting, and improvement of infrastructure and transportation. Other issues are undertaken by both TBR and TLA as interests develop among their members.

I am still pushing for improvements in the community. This is where I began my civic and political journey, and I intend to continue working to better our community and the state of Louisiana for as long as my health will allow. My current efforts include my commitment to the fight for fair election maps in Louisiana, using the federal suit *Robinson v. Landry* (originally *Robinson v. Ardoin*), in which I am the lead plaintiff. As I draw these recollections to a close, it seems I have come full circle. I feel that I can validate the adage—from an optimistic angle this time—the more things change, the more they stay the same.

SOURCES

Note: I relied heavily on the *Advocate* newspaper to fill in details of various recollections. For many years that paper was published for the Baton Rouge area in morning and afternoon editions, the *Morning Advocate* and *State-Times,* as well as a Sunday edition. The older editions are now referred to in many online archives as the *State-Times Advocate*. This accounts for the variety of newspaper titles listed below.

"About the AAUP." AAUP, 11 Dec. 2020, https://www.aaup.org/about-aaup.
Adams, Art. "Claudel Wins School Board Ward 2 Seat." *Morning Advocate,* 8 Nov. 1972.
———. "School Board Says Little on Revamp." *Morning Advocate,* 10 Mar. 1972.
Adams, Gibbs, and Ed Cullen. "Judge Denies Motions for New Trial." *Morning Advocate,* 14 Nov. 1974.
"Advocates Applaud Fifth Circuit's Denial of State's Request for Reconsideration in *Robinson v. Ardoin*." ACLU of Louisiana, 15 Dec. 2023.
American Federation of Teachers, https://www.aft.org/.
"Annexation Said Better for Scotlandville Now." *State-Times Advocate,* 12 July 1977.
"Baker Wins Right to Set Up Its Own School System." *The Advocate,* 31 Dec. 1995.
Ballard, Mark. "Baton Rouge Community College Opens Monday." *The Advocate,* 16 Aug. 2020.
Bartels, Paul. "City Council Okays Annexation of North Park Shopping Center." *Morning Advocate,* 27 Feb. 1975.

SOURCES

———. "North Park Shopping Center Asks to Be Part of City of Baton Rouge." *Morning Advocate,* 22 Jan. 1975.

Baton Rouge Community College Management Council. *The School of Choice—A Choice of a Lifetime—School Catalog.* Baton Rouge, LA, 1998.

Blue, Jason L., director. *Otis' Dream.* Trinity United Church of Christ, 2020, https://www.otisdream.com/.

"Board Gives Support to SU Administration." *Morning Advocate,* 17 Nov. 1972.

"BR Legal Aid Society to Consolidate Offices." *State-Times Advocate,* 21 Jan. 1975.

Buchanan, Don. "Scotlandville Vote Explained." *State-Times Advocate,* 8 Feb. 1972.

"Citizen Turnout Is Small for Charter Change Meet." *State-Times,* 30 Jan. 1974.

"Close Look Urged on Incorporation of Scotlandville." *State-Times Advocate,* 18 Feb. 1974.

Collins, Robert. "Local Newsman Gives SU Eyewitness Account." *Morning Advocate,* 17 Nov. 1972.

"Committee Seek Successor to SU President." *Morning Advocate,* 16 Nov. 1973.

"Cooperative Membership Meeting Set." *Morning Advocate,* 6 Nov. 1973.

Cotton, George. "Clash Leaves 2 Dead." *Morning Advocate,* 17 Nov. 1972.

———. "Conflict, Confusion Mar Meeting." *Morning Advocate,* 4 May 1975.

———. "Opponents of Stone to 'Wait and See.'" *Morning Advocate,* 22 Feb. 1974.

———. "SU Presidency Search Panel Gives Views on Only 3 of 15 Applicants." *Morning Advocate,* 17 Feb. 1974.

"Demo Panel Candidate Gives Views." *Morning Advocate,* 2 Oct. 1975.

Dickinson, Larry. "CC73 Article Would Hike Home Rule Powers in LA." *State-Times Advocate,* 9 Feb. 1974.

———. "Sweeping Home Rule Powers Contained in CC73 Article." *State-Times Advocate,* 8 Feb. 1974.

Didier, Karen. "Spikes Eyes Major Changes for Southern." *Morning Advocate,* 2 Nov. 1988.

"Discrimination Suit Is Filed." *State-Times Advocate,* 4 Aug. 1975.

Drone, Donald. "If School Board Member Won't Push for Quality Everywhere." *The Advocate,* 17 Sept. 2020.

Dunne, Mike. "Discontent Fueled CAPE." *The Advocate,* 10 Nov. 1994.

———. "School Board Members Take Oath, Vow Unity." *The Advocate,* 19 Dec. 1994.

———. "The School Board's 19 Rules for Success." *The Advocate,* 24 Jan. 1995.

SOURCES

Dyer, Scott. "Gov. Foster Wants to Restructure Higher Education System." *The Advocate*, 13 Jan. 1996.

———. "Jefferson Pulls Strings to Get SUNO Position." *The Advocate*, 8 Dec. 1998.

———. "Legard Wins School Board Presidency on Second Vote." *State-Times*, 11 Jan. 1991.

———. "SU Alumnus May Lead Community College." *The Advocate*, 17 Oct. 1995.

"EBR Voters to Consider Remapping." *State-Times*, 1 Dec. 1971.

Editorial. "Drennen Wrong in Site Selection." *State-Times*, 17 Aug. 1996.

"E-W Runway Construction Halt Is Asked." *Morning Advocate*, 18 Aug. 1967.

Eysink, Curt. "Board's Battles Exhausted Talbot." *The Advocate*, 14 July 1991.

"Federal Appeals Court Defines Desegregation Law Exemptions." *Morning Advocate*, 7 Sept. 1967.

Foreman, Yvonne G. "Robinson Says Legal Aid Unit Report Contains Constructive Criticisms." *Morning Advocate*, 23 Nov. 1977.

Francalancia, Angie. "Stone Wants 3-Year SU Contract." *Morning Advocate*, 27 Oct. 1984.

"Freemasonry." Britannica, https://www.britannica.com/topic/Freemasonry.

Fryer, Milford. "School Board Seeks Lifting of Desegregation Gag Order." *Morning Advocate*, 22 July 1981.

Garland, Greg. "Screen Picks Tom Woods as Fire Chief." *State-Times Advocate*, 27 May 1987.

"Geddes Wins Over Belton." *Morning Advocate*, 4 Nov. 1970.

"A Glorious Past, A Brighter Future." *The Torch* (Morehouse College yearbook), 1957.

"Grab Ryan Airport for Baton Rouge, Urges Councilman." *Morning Advocate*, 7 Jan. 1975.

"Holiday for King May Be Best Now." *State-Times Advocate*, 6 Oct. 1987.

Jackson, Curtis. "Theodore Martin Alexander Sr. (1909–2001)" Find a Grave, 1 Nov. 2001. https://www.findagrave.com/memorial/120086898/theodore-martin-alexander.

Jones, Terry. "After 20 Years, Hope Building for a Neighborhood Grocery Store." *The Advocate*, 28 May 2019.

Judd, Angela. "10 Tips for How to Grow Corn." *Growing in the Garden*, Mediavine Home, 14 Jan. 2021. https://growinginthegarden.com/how-to-grow-corn-10-tips-for-growing-corn/.

SOURCES

"Labor Board Spokesman Declares Probe into Acme Brick Not Begun." *Morning Advocate,* 5 Mar. 1969.

"Lawrence E. Moch Sr. Dead at 61." *The Advocate,* 28 Dec. 1990.

"Legal Aid Society Board Restructuring Proposed." *State-Times Advocate,* 28 Feb. 1978.

Lightfoot, Linda. "Boudreaux Reprimand Is Ignored." *State-Times,* 30 Sept. 1970.

Lussier, Charles. "50 Years after Desegregation Order." *The Advocate,* 28 Nov. 2020.

———. "Out-of-State Billionaires Donating to EBR School Board Races." *The Advocate,* 3 Dec. 2018.

Lussier, Charles. "Robinson Says He Predicted System Breakup." *The Advocate,* 19 Apr. 2013.

"Man Meted Term for Possession of Hashish." *Morning Advocate,* 27 Sept. 1975.

McClain, Randy. "Blacks Eye Roles on School Board." *Morning Advocate,* 14 Sept. 1980.

———. "Board Gets More Time on Mix Plan." *Morning Advocate,* 4 Oct. 1980.

———. "School Board Asks Early Seating of Blacks." *Morning Advocate,* 24 Oct. 1980.

McKee, Don. "Many Southerners Believe Racial Crisis Has Passed." *Morning Advocate,* 1 Oct. 1964.

McMahon, Bill. "Board Single-Member District Bill Gets House Panel's Support." *State-Times Advocate,* 20 May 1977.

———. "Panel Names Jesse Stone Next Southern President." *Morning Advocate,* 21 Feb. 1974.

———. "Scotlandville Issue Looms before Voters." *Morning Advocate,* 1 Dec. 1971.

———. "Voters League Talks Pros, Cons of Scotlandville Incorporation." *Morning Advocate,* 18 Dec. 1971

Miller, Robert G. "Pontchartrain Park Seeks Spot on Register." *New Orleans Times-Picayune,* 2 Nov. 2003.

———. "SUNO's Biology Department Is Thriving." *New Orleans Times-Picayune,* 15 Dec. 2002.

Moller, Jan. "Kerry Returns to Louisiana to Shore Up Demo Support." *New Orleans Times- Picayune,* 8 May 2004.

Morris, John. "Scotlandville Self-Gov't Feasible, Turnley Says." *State-Times,* 12 Nov. 1974.

SOURCES

"Museum Studies—Mission, Vision and Core Values." Southern University System, https://www.suno.edu/search?q=Museum+Studies.

"New Communities Issue Is Revived." *Morning Advocate*, 22 June 1993.

Pack, William. "Desegregation Plan Meeting 'Productive.'" *The Advocate*, 28 Dec. 1995.

Pearson, Drew. "The Washington Merry Go Round." *Morning Advocate*, 31 Dec. 1964.

"Press Robinson Runs for EBR School Board." *Morning Advocate*, 14 July 1976.

"Production Workers." *The Advocate*, 24 Feb. 1969.

"Richard Turnley Runs for House." *The Advocate*, 2 Aug. 1971.

Robinson v. Ardoin, 605 F. Supp. 3d 759-2022.

Ruth, Dawn. "SUNO Chancellor Spends First Day on Introductions." *New Orleans Times-Picayune*, 2 July 1987.

Sanders, Hosea, and Marsha Jordan. "'Otis' Dream' Indie Film Produced by Chicago Church Lauded by Critics." *ABC7 Chicago*, WLS-TV, 14 Oct. 2021, https://abc7chicago.com/otis-dream-movie-otis-moss/11112965/.

Sapp, Sherry. "Community College May Lease Space for First Year." *The Advocate*, 25 July 1996.

"School Board Votes to Ask Council for Permit at Ryan." *State-Times Advocate*, 31 May 1968.

"Scope Food Store Sets Grand Opening Saturday." *Morning Advocate*, 1 Dec. 1972.

"Scope Reports Enrollments of 420." *State-Times Advocate*, 24 Aug. 1972.

"Scotlandville Scope Co-Op Store to Open." *State-Times Advocate*, 1 Dec. 1972.

Seghers, Frances. "Annexation Petition Seems to Dim Scotlandville Incorporation Efforts." *Morning Advocate*, 28 July 1976.

———. "City Council Annexes More Area to City." *Morning Advocate*, 23 Dec. 1976.

———. "Scot'ville Annexation Approved." *Morning Advocate*, 26 Oct. 1978.

Sentell, Will. "Advocates Praise Bills Allowing LA Families to Pick Schools." *The Advocate*, 7 Mar. 2022.

"Southern Promotes Press Robinson." *Sunday Advocate*, 28 July 1991.

"Striking Acme Co. Workers Get Support of Two Groups." *The Advocate*, 26 Feb. 1969.

SU Faculty Senate. "SU Faculty Senate Newsletter." Baton Rouge, LA, 1973.

SOURCES

"SU Group Delays Truck Halt Plan." *The Advocate*, 27 Feb. 1969.

"SU–Shreveport Gets New Chancellor." *The Advocate*, 17 Nov. 2000.

"Text of Judge Parker's Ruling in Federal Court." *Morning Advocate*, 13 June 1981.

"Three Negroes Selected Local Legal Aid Directors." *Morning Advocate*, 7 Dec. 1966.

Tillman, T. C. "E-W Runway Effort Dropped by Council." *The Advocate*, 27 June 1968.

Together Baton Rouge, https://www.togetherbr.org/.

Together Louisiana, https://www.togetherla.org/.

The Torch. Yearbook of Morehouse College, 1957.

Warren, Chante Dionne. "Kelley, Smith, Pratt Win Seats on School Board." *The Advocate*, 9 Nov. 1994.

———. "Prejean Recalls SU Demonstrations." *The Advocate*, 24 Feb. 1996.

"What Is an HBCU?" White House Initiative on Advancing Educational Equity . . ., https://sites.ed.gov/whhbcu/one-hundred-and-five-historically-black-colleges-and-universities/.

"Would Appear That Politics, Not Racism Is the Bottom Line." *The Advocate*, 5 May 1987.

INDEX

Note: Page numbers in italic denote illustrations.

A. Philip Randolph Institute, 94
American Association of University Professors (AAUP), 62
Acme Brick strike, 78–80
Adegboye, Dr. David, 163–64
Aertker, Robert, 120
Airline Terrace subdivision, 89–90
Albert, Mitchell, Jr., 85, 94
Alexander, Theodore Martin, Sr., 41
Allen, Henry, 86, 92
Allen, Marvin, 150
Alpha Phi Alpha fraternity, 40, 44, 119, 170
American Chemical Society, 173
American Federation of Teachers (AFT), 62–63
Amiss, Sheriff Al, 61, 84–85
Anderson, Gerard A., 19
Anna T. Jordan Park, 73
Anna T. Jordan Recreational Council, 94
Armstrong, Willie C., 150
Arveson, Raymond, 137
Atlanta University Center, 33
Aull, Herbert E. (Hots), 119

Austin, Samuel, 63
Avery, Donald, 115

Banks subdivision, 89–90
Banks, Chauna, 93
Bankston, Mildred C., 118
Barnes, Myrtis, 94
Barnes, William T., 40
Bashful, Emmett W., 166
Baton Rouge Community College (BRCC), 153–54, 155
Baucom, Joyce, 63
Bell, Fred, Jr., vii, 29, 45, 170
Bellar, Martin, 84
Bellemont Motor Lodge, 52
Belton, Acie, 77, 82, 87, 117, 118, 120
Belton, Ada, 63
Belton, Ray L., 158
Beta Kappa Chi, 173
Bibbins, Jody, 78
Birkett, Dr. Brenda, 151
Black, "Buckskin" Bill, 147
Blanco, Gov. Kathleen, 144
Boger, Dellie L., 39, 40
Bonaparte, Dr. Marion, 153
Bouie, Dr. Joseph, 157, 159, 162, 165

INDEX

Bowen, A. L., 63
Brady, U.S. District Judge James, 135
Branch, Mike, 142–44, 147
Brazeal, Brailsford, 39
Breda, William, 109, 137–40
Brew, Ferguson, 85
Brisbane, Robert H., Jr., 39
Broome, Mayor-Pres. Sharon Weston, 92
Brown, John, 63, 94
Brown, District Judge William, 137
Brown, Leonard Douglas, 61
Bryant, Dr. D'Orsay, 79, 118
Burns, District Atty. Prem, 116
Bursh, Talmadge, 54

Carnahan, Carolyn Woodfin, 175
Carter, Hezekiah, 80
Chisolm, Shirley, 95
Christenson, Sabinus H., 39
Civil Rights Act of 1964, 52, 129, 131
Claflin College, 30
Clark College, 33, 38
Clark, Dr. Felton G., 63, 153
Clarke, Wilbur B., 51, 53, 54, 129, 130, 131
Clarke, Neola, 53
Claudel, J. O., 118–19, 123
Cochran, Johnnie, Jr., 168
Collier, Clarence Marie, 65
Community Advancement, Inc. (CAI), 72–74, 90, 94
Community Against Drugs and Violence, 93
Community Association for the Welfare of School Children, 94
Congress of Racial Equality (CORE), 54
Cormier, Maxine, 95
Courtney, John, 79
Couvillion, Lawrence, 152
Craig, Diane, 153
Crawford, Robert, 132, 133, 141

Creary, Ansel, 63, 67
Cross, Mike, 144
Cunningham, Clarence, 85
Cunningham, Edsel, 115
Cyrus, Rev. Leo, 147

Dabbs, George, 126
Dansby, Claude B. "Pop," 39
Davis, Leroy, 63
DeJean, Preston, 153
Delgado Community College, 154
Delpit, State Rep. Joseph A. ("Joe"), 66, 73, 77, 84, 96, 115, 120–21
Democratic State Central Committee of Louisiana (DSCC), 93, 94–95
Devall, Jay, 144
Doomes, Dr. Earl, 54
Douglas, Emmitt C., 77
Drennen, Mark, 155
Duke, David, 143
Dukes, Jerome, 52
Dumas, Mayor W. W. "Woody," 73, 76, 90
Dumas, Walter, 65, 95, 121
Dunne, Mike, 147
Duplichain University, 172–73
Dyson, Larry, 77

Eames, George Washington, 119, 141
East Baton Rouge Human Relations Council, 94
East, Sen. John Porter, 144
East Baton Rouge Parish School System (EBRPSS), 128
Echols, Dr. Richard, 54
Eden Park, 72, 96, 118, 121, 122
Edwards, Gov. Edwin W., 61, 65, 85–86, 111, 119, 120
Edwards, James H. "Chick," 94
Edwards, Gov. John Bel, 61

INDEX

Ellison, James B., 32
Erickson, John, 146

Faculty Senate (Southern University), 63–64, 67, 97–98, 160, 161, 162
Fields, Cleo, 97
First Ward Voters League, 77, 79
Flemming, Wilton, 54
Florida Boulevard, 92–93, 116
Floyd, Raymond, 63
Fluker, Lt. Thomas, 85
Fontenot, Patrick, 153
food deserts, 92–93
Food Town Supermarket & Ethical Pharmacy, 90–91
Ford, Robert, 67
Foster, Gov. Murphy (Mike), 61, 155, 156
Fowler, Sue, 133
Francis, Dr. Norman C., 169
Freemasonry, 4, 52
Friends of CAPE, 146
Fun Fair Park, 131

Geddes, J. Clyde, 117
Geller, Melvin "Coach," 119
George, Pearl, 73, 77
Gex, Dr. Robert, 165
Gogreve, Donald J., 148
Goodwin, Randall, 124
Graham, Ira, 63
Granger, Charlie, 73
Green, Rev. H. P., 118
"grocery gaps," 92

Hammatt, Noel, 147
Hammonds, Robert, *109*, 134
Harding Boulevard, 52, 53, 96
Harding Elementary School, 77, 124
Hardnett, Charlene, 60

Hardy, Dr. Henry, 161
Harley, Lawrence, 47
Harris, Aaron, 63
Harrison, Dr. E. C., 51, 64, 161
Harrison, Lonnie, 32
Harvey, Steve, 157
Hayes, Dewey, 87–88
Hearn, Etta Kay, *103*
Hearn, Redell, 164
Helms, Jesse, 144
Henderson, Dan, 147, 148
Hicks, Margery, 94
Hightower, Louis, 35–36
Hill, Rickey, 60
Holden, Melvin "Kip," 96
Holliday, Jensen, 146
Holloway, Ms., 15–16
Holmes, Frances, 63
Honore, Dalton, 85
Hope, John, 63, 74
Houghton, Joan, 123–24
Howard University, vii, 38, 43–46, 50
Hudson, Dr. Charles, 85
Human Jukebox (Southern), 172
Humphrey, Hubert, 95
Hutchinson, Gordon, 142
Hymel, Judge L. J., 115

Interstate 110 (I-110), 80, 82
Isaiah, Eugene ("Gene"),
Isaiah, Malikiah ("Mallie"), 32

Jackson, Audrey, 74
Jackson, Edward R., 151, 153
Jackson, Jesse, 95
Jackson, Luvenia, 27
Jackson, McHenry, 58
Jacobs, Carolyn, 63
Jefferson, Andrea, 159

INDEX

Jefferson, Dr. Jack, 54
Jefferson, William, *113*, 157, 168
Jetson, Louis, 82
Johnson, Clyde, 63
Johnson, Lyndon B., 72, 130
Johnson, Mack, 51–52
Johnson, O. Clayton, 153
Johnson, Rev. Lionel, Sr., 65, 66
Johnston, J. Bennett, 143
Jones, Clarence, 140
Jones, Dr. Edward A., 39
Jones, Essie, 51
Jones, Johnnie A., 84, 94
Jones, Robert L., 98
Jordan, Edward "Kidd," 163
Joseph, Kenneth, 86, 94

Kelley, Ingrid, 147
Kennedy, Audrey, 82
Kerry, Sen. John, *113*, 168
Khruschev, Nikita, 44
King, Bazella, 25
King, Booker T., 25
King, Booker T., Jr., 25
King, Dr. Martin Luther, Jr., 30, 44, 50, 144–46
Kyle, Dan, 160

LaFleur, Martial J., 120
Lawson, Belford, 44
Ledoux, Eldon, 147
Lee, James W., Jr., 85
Legal Aid Society of Baton Rouge (LAS), 82–84
Legard, Eva, *106*, 122, 123
Leland, Mickey, 97
Lewis, Clayton, 94, 151
Lincoln Hotel, 52
Lincoln Theater, 52

Livors, Sam, 117
Louisiana Academy of Sciences, 173
Louisiana Campus Compact (LACC), 168
Lussier, Charles, 127

Mandela, Nelson, 157
March on Washington, 50
Marsellus, Howard, 73, 120
Marsh, Frances, 63
Marshall, Franz, 138
Marshall, Thurgood, 44
Martin, Dr. Julia, 54, 55, 63
Martin, Wade O., 118, 120
Masingale, Eula, 63
Masonic Hall (Scotlandville), 52
Mays, Dr. Benjamin Elijah, 30–32
McBay, Henry C., 33, 39
McCastle, Lionel, 80
McCleary, Mike, *104*, 132–33
McClinton, Flandus, 151
McClure, Dr. Wesley Cornelious, 153
McDonald, Moses, 53
McGovern, George, 95
McHenry, Albert, 63
McKeithen, Gov. John, 79, 158
McKinley High School, 109, 137–40
McNairy, Dr. Sidney, 54
Melrose Bowling Lane, 130–31
Merrick, Robyn, 153
Milledgeville, GA, 38
Miller, Basile, 66
Miller, Dr. Robert, 54
Miller, Patricia B., 131
Millican, Frank, 122, 123, 138, 139, 141–42, 145
Mims, Jacqueline, 146, 147–48
Minority Engineers of Louisiana, Inc. (MEL), 68–71, 162
Moch, Lawrence E., Sr., 119
Montgomery, T. H., 133, 142

INDEX

Montgomery, AL, 51
Moore, Dr. William, 54, 63, 150, 151
Moran, Robert, 63
Moreco's Lounge, 52, 53
Morehouse College ("the House"), vii, 30–43, 44, 48
Morgan State University, 48
Morris Brown College, 33
Morris, Dr. Kelso B., 48–49, 54
Moser, Roger, 147
Moss, Otis, Sr., 42
Moye, Allen J., 94
Mueller, Dr. P. S., 46
Municipal Fire and Police Civil Service Board, 176

NAACP, 41, 54, 77, 79, 108, 128, 133, 140, 141, 148–49
National Conference of Christians and Jews (NCCJ), 175
National Conference for Community and Justice, 175
National Council for Accreditation of Teacher Education (NCATE), 160–61, 166
National Institutes of Health, 46
National Urban League, 54
Nelson, Dr. Ivory, 54
Netterville, Dr. G. Leon, 60, 61, 120, 153
Newman, Jewel J., 73, 86, 90, 94, 95
Nichols, Lloyd, 63
Nissan-ETS Fellows Program, 162
Nixon, Brenda, 120
North Baton Rouge, 81, 93
Nunez Community College, 154

Odell, Albert C., 122
Old South Baton Rouge, 92
Osborn, Fr. Aubry, 57

Packer, Dan, 169
Park Vista, 58–59, 94
Park Vista Improvement Association (PVIA), 58–59
Parker, Judge John V., 121, 123, 125–26, 135, 148
Parker, Wiley W., 51
Parrish, Janet, 146
Paul, Leo, 131
Paul, Chief Murphy J., Jr., 176–77
Payne, Lillie, 91
Peoples, Gerald, 159, 165
Perdue, Wiley, 40
Perkins, Huel D., 64
Peterson, Dan, 63
Phi Beta Kappa, 173
Pinsonat, Bernie, 146
Pitcher, Judge Freddie, Jr., 116, 147
Pitts, Matthew, 73
Plank Bowl, 130
Plank Road, 77, 88, 96, 97, 115
Popleon, Ed, 73
Pounds, Janet, 54
Pratt, Warren, 147
Prejean, Fred, 60, 61–62
Prescott, James D., 132
Prescott, Sarah Edwina, *103*, 132
Prestage, Dr. James J., 64, 153
Prince Hall Masons, 4, 52

Rabon, William P., 148
Reilly, Kevin, 73
Reynolds, William Bradford, 138
Rhodes, Thornton, 54, 131
Rivers, Griffin, 85
Robinson v. Landry (formerly *Robinson v. Ardoin*), viii, 177–78
Robinson, Dr. William, 54
Robinson, Press, Jr. (son), 57

INDEX

Robinson, Prince, Jr. (father), 1, 2, 3–4, 9–10, 13–14, 16, 17–18, 19, 20–22, 24, 25, 27, 28, 30, 36, 43, 47, 57–58

Robinson, Robin Sean (son), 57

Robinson, Ruth Ann (née Washington) (wife), 56–58, *114*, 170

Robinson, Viola (née Isaiah) (mother), 1, 2, 3–4, 6–7, 9–10, 13–14, 16, 18, 19, 21, 22, 23, 24, 36, 43, 47

Roman, Malik, 60

Roquemore, Leroy, 63

Rose, Doretha, *103*

Ruffin, Dr. Spaulding, 54, 63

Ryan Airport, 76–77, 88, 89

Ryan Elementary School, 76

Salters, Alma, 35

Sanders, Evans, 79

Savoie, Joseph, 168

Scenic Highway, 53, 77, 78, 80, 90, 91, 96

Scotlandville, LA, 51, 52, 57, 72–78, 80–82, 87–93, 94, 96–97, 98, 117, 118, 121, 122

Scotlandville Advisory Council (SAC), 72–73, 74

Scotlandville Area Advisory Council (SAAC), 74–98, 116, 122–24

Scotlandville Cooperative of Food Entrepreneurs (SCOPE), 90–92

Scotlandville Food Cooperative, 91–94

Scotlandville-Zion City Area Board of Community Advancement, 94

Scott, Geraldine, 63

Scott, Raymond P., 77

Screen, Mayor-Pres. Pat, 86

Second Ward Voters League, 77, 87, 89–90, 117

Sells, Dr. Rose Duhon, 161, 172

Shereshefsky, Dr. J. L., 45

Shortess, Judge Melvin, 89

Sigma Xi, 173

Simon, Ernest, 63, 131

Sims, Percy, 73

Slaughter, Ralph, 153

Smalley, Dr. Arnold, 54

Smalley, Dr. Mildred, 54

Smith, Denver Allen, 61

Smith, Dr. Valerian, 56, 57

Smith, Frances, 153

Smith, Herman, 64

Smith, Patricia Haynes, 147

Smith, Rev. Charles T., 146

South Baton Rouge, 72, 77, 94, 96, 117, 118, 121, 122

South Baton Rouge Advisory Committee, 117

Southern Association of Colleges and Schools (SACS), 173

Southern Bowling Congress (SBC), 131

Southern Christian Leadership Conference (SCLC), 54

Southern Heights, 58, 89–90

Southern University, viii, 36, 46, 48, 51, 54, 55, 56, 58, 60–71, 78, 83, 88, 90, 96, 97–98, 115, 119, 152, 153–56, 157–70, 172

Southern University New Orleans (SUNO), viii, 61, *112*, *113*, 134, 149, 150–52, 154, 157, 159–65, 166–70

Southern University at Shreveport, Louisiana (SUSLA, formerly Southern University Shreveport-Bossier [SUSBO]), 156, 157–59

Spelman College, 33, 38

Spikes, Dolores, 63, 97–98, 150, 153, 156

Spikes, Hermon, 98

Steptoe, Dr. Roosevelt, 88, 96, 153

Sternberg, Josef, 175

INDEX

Stewart, Dr. William, 162
Stewart, Henry, III, 63
Stone, Dr. Jesse N., 64–67, 153
Student Nonviolent Coordinating
  Committee (SNCC), 54

Talbot, Jim, *106*, 137–39, 141–42
Tapp, Charlie W., 72–73
Tarver, Cynthia, 151
Tarver, Dr. Leon R., II, *113*, 152, 153, 157, 158, 159–60, 165, 169
Taylor, Cleve, 88, 90
Temple Theater/Roof, 52
Thomas Road, 88
Thomas, Charlie, Jr., 140
Thompson, Gloria, 160
Tiensu, Dr. Victor, 55
Tillman, Celestine, 55
Together Baton Rouge (TBR), 92–93, 177
Together Louisiana, 176, 177
Tolson, Roslyn, 63
Triangle Lounge, 52, 53
Trotman, Charles, 55
Turner, Harold, 94
Turner, Sue Wilbert, 175
Turnley, Richard, 66, 72, 73, 77, 84, 86, 88, 92, 94, 95, 96, 97, 115, 117, 120–21

United Citizens for Community Action, 94

Valley Park neighborhood, 81, 116
Vaughn, J. W., 85
Vincent, Beverly, 134

Wartell, George, 36
Washington, Alvin, 149
Watson, Morgan M., 69–70
Wells, Clara Mae, 119, 122
Wells, Wally W., 124
Wesley, Lee, 73
West, Judge E. Gordon, 118, 120
Whalum, Wendell P., 39, 40
Whisenton, Dr. Joffre T., 97, 153
White, Dr. Vandon, 48, 51, 55
White, Tolar, 151, 153
Whitfield, Dr. George, 85
Wilcox, Thomas J., Jr., 63
Williams, Eddie, 4–5, 36
Williams, Edith, 5, 36
Williams, Frank, 63
Williams, Lynn, 5, 36
Williams, Margie, 5, 36
Williams, Robert, *109*, 139
Williams, Ruthie Lee, 3, 4–5, 6, 7, 20–21, 32, 36
Williams, Samuel W., 39
Williams, T. T., 92
Wilson High School, vii, 19, 27, 28, 30
Wilson, James, 92
Wisham, Mary, 106
Woodaire subdivision, 89–90
Woods, Thomas, 86
Woolco (North Park) Shopping Center, 88, 89

Yates, Dr. Marvin, 153

Zion City, 94

Printed in the USA
CPSIA information can be obtained
at www.ICGtesting.com
CBHW030723150724
11513CB00019BA/460/J

9 780807 182819